Lean Six Sigma for the Practitioner

Lean Six Sigma for the Practitioner

The Hows and Whys of Process Improvement

Dino Pupulin

IGUANA

Copyright © 2017 Dino Pupulin
Published by Iguana Books
720 Bathurst Street, Suite 303
Toronto, Ontario, Canada
M5S 2R4

Publisher: Mary Ann J. Blair
Editor: Mary Ann J. Blair
Front cover image: woman opening door (iStock); paper pinned to wall (Shutterstock)
Front cover design: Jessica Albert
Book layout design: Meghan Behse

Library and Archives Canada Cataloguing in Publication

Pupulin, Dino, 1967-, author
    Lean Six Sigma for the Practitioner : The Hows and Whys of Process Improvement / Dino Pupulin

Issued in print format.
ISBN 978-1-77180-225-3

1. Process control. 2. Lean manufacturing. 3. Six sigma (Quality control standard). I. Title.

TS156.8.P86 2017   658.5   C2017-904663-2
                                C2017-904664-0

This is an original print edition of *Lean Six Sigma for the Practitioner.*

Contents

To all those who get it

Chapter 1

Introduction

Today is the day! The consultants with their crisp suits and million-dollar smiles have invaded the boardroom and are about to execute an ambush. This is the day that the company will decide to adopt Lean or Six Sigma or Lean/Six Sigma. As much as you want to make the right investment by bringing in "experts," the implementation will likely fail if your decision is based only on a consultant's recommendation. A successful Lean/Six Sigma implementation is less a function of the consultants you've hired and more a function of the people in your organization. Take the time to understand your own people who will be able to lead the change and let that information guide what sort of process improvement is necessary and how to approach it. The consultants will not do this for you, and at the end of the project the consultants will be gone.

Mix Lean Tools, Not Organizational Levels

The concept of lean (now applied well beyond just manufacturing) has been known for years as a way to reduce material costs, reduce labour costs per part, reduce inventory costs, and improve quality. The beauty of the concept is that you can implement it in your own company without a lot of outside help. You can take measures to reduce inventory (often by half), reduce waste (and costs by extension), and better deploy labour to take advantage of savings or increased customer response.

However, once you have decided that your company is ripe for a more formal process-improvement initiative, the decisions become harder. As I've indicated thus far, process improvement comes in many forms, with Lean/Six Sigma being the most recent, and although the initial question appears to be whether to adopt Lean, Six Sigma, or its hybrid, Lean/Six Sigma, the real question should be "Who in my organization has the most impact on what the customer gets?" That question will tell you the level where you should begin.

Lean promises low levels of just-in-time inventory and zero waste. Six Sigma promises low process variability and a focus on the voice of the customer. Activity-based costing promises proper cost allocation. Theory of constraints offers coordinated bottleneck management. Business process reengineering promises an employee sense of responsibility. All of these ideas seem beneficial and there do not appear to be any limitations or conflicts between them. If we could choose to implement all of them, we would!

To some extent you can do just that. The tools to implement these process-improvement regimes are often transferable, so you can use lean tools in Six Sigma and vice versa. Such flexibility is the nature of Lean/Six Sigma. However, these process-improvement regimes differ on philosophical level and thus require more exploration.

The Concept of Lean

Lean is a concept that helps manufacturing and service companies increase their profitability and competitiveness. When a company *goes lean*, it identifies and improves a design or operations process so that its product or service reaches the customer in perfect form in the shortest possible time.

I have extensive experience with two different process-improvement regimes: Lean Manufacturing and Six Sigma. These regimes have a lot in common, but each has a different focus and uses different practices or tools. In this book, I will provide you, the decision maker, with everything you need to understand these regimes in order to make a sound decision about whether and how to undertake a process-improvement initiative in your company. Although I approach process improvement with an open mind as to where it will eventually go, my experience has been mostly Lean

Manufacturing and Six Sigma, and the best and most numerous examples in this book will be from those regimes. Nevertheless, this book will be helpful to you regardless of how you decide to approach process improvement.

Simplified Lean History

The first recognized lean implementation was the Toyota Production System in Japan under the guidance of Taiichi Onho. In the late 1980s and early 1990s, I was working for General Motors, then the biggest company in the world. I saw Toyota go from having an insignificant world-market share to being so successful that Chrysler (the number three automotive company in the world) argued it could successfully compete with the Japanese only with government help.

At first, the management at General Motors saw lean manufacturing as a couple of simple tricks whose value would disappear. But, during my tenure there, I saw it go from being seen as a futile diversion to the thing that would save the company. After I left General Motors, the push to lean manufacturing by all of the American automotive plants increased, but they never seemed to catch up with Toyota. The ironic thing is that lean did not come about because Toyota or Japan had any fundamental advantage in the market. Japan had no input advantages or notable strength to facilitate this incredible rise. In fact, lean did not rely on any factor advantages, but was instead a direct response to Toyota's lack of advantages.

The fact that Toyota used lean manufacturing to go from having no advantages to being the biggest car company in the world means that anyone can do the same thing in any industry regardless of advantages. Even you can do this.

Common Mistakes in Implementing Process Improvement

For the last two decades, I have worked for or with companies that have initiated process improvement, and it is surprising how many decision makers overcomplicate this exceedingly simple decision.

As a reader, you should be given an opportunity to avoid the same mistakes. I wrote this book for you — to help you make sense of process improvement so you can secure its benefits.

Companies make two common mistakes when implementing process improvement. The first occurs *when decision makers think they will single-handedly turn around their company by making the decision.* True, at some point there needs to be a leadership decision to implement a process-improvement regime (including deciding which one), but the success of the initiative rests on there already being enough improvement *traction* in the company. If a company is not ready, an all-in decision is often more detrimental than helpful. Because readiness is fundamental to success, I do not discuss the strategic decision at the corporate level until later in this book. Many benefits should be accrued and cultural understanding acquired before making a decision to implement a process-improvement regime, and a decision maker should take care not to squelch such benefits by making a top-down decision.

The second common mistake is *assuming that all process-improvement regimes are the same.* This is easy to do because the *tools* are interchangeable, and even I treat process- improvement regimes interchangeably from time to time in this book. Their *philosophies*, however, are not interchangeable. In fact, they are quite distinct, and picking one over another involves costly trade-offs. Understanding the philosophical differences and trade-offs is extremely important when deciding whether to implement Lean Manufacturing, Six Sigma, some other regime, or even your own production system. People speak of "Lean Six Sigma" as if it were one regime, but the two regimes align only in their training offerings.

Philosophically, each regime targets a different part of the organization for improvement, so first you need to know which part of your organization has the biggest impact on what the customer receives. Taiichi Onho, who introduced the concept of lean at Toyota, thought the operator had the biggest influence, so the operator is the focus of lean manufacturing. By contrast, Six Sigma types at Allied Signal (and later Motorola) thought that product and process design had the biggest impact, so they targeted engineers and designers rather than operators. At some point in a process-improvement initiative, projects will focus on either the operator or the designer and thus be either Lean or Six Sigma projects. If the focus of your process-improvement initiative is not clear, mixing Lean projects with Six Sigma projects will pull the company in different directions, something I learned when I worked at Seagate Technology.

Lean Applies Worldwide

Even after decision makers identify one clear focus for a process-improvement initiative, they can still go wrong, especially if they insist that what they're doing is novel or if they invest their improvement with special powers without understanding what it is intended to do.

When I worked at General Motors in the 1990s, the company put a big effort into this "new" idea called lean manufacturing. People at my plant were sent to see W. Edwards Deming read from his book. Deming was a respected authority in the quality movement and an inspiration for the Toyota success that was later called "lean," but no one who attended learned anything that would make a practical difference at General Motors. As part of implementing lean manufacturing, I was assigned to create light boards that would tell forklift drivers where to go next. I don't think that forklift drivers ever got lost before that time, at least not on purpose, but somehow this new light board was supposed to improve efficiency. I also witnessed a debate between a colleague and management about whether layout mattered (U-cells versus line flow) if neither configuration made a difference to quality. The lean expert took my colleague's side and affirmed that any changes were supposed to result in improvements instead of being ends in and of themselves. I did not understand any of this, however, until years later when I realized that General Motors was doing lean wrong.

It was not until I worked at Ernst & Young as a consultant that I saw a clear picture. Thankfully, I worked with some exceptionally smart people who helped me turn my misguided experience at General Motors into the hows and whys of lean, and then I realized that it was an exceptionally useful process-improvement regime. I got plenty of experience implementing lean, and my clients were very happy with the outcomes. Despite the bad start at General

Motors, I never considered lean to be something new and novel. Instead, I saw it as something obvious that just took a little while to clarify. Through practice and seeing a lot of its varied uses, I became very comfortable with its notions and methodology. It just became "the way you do things if you want to do them right."

My convictions about lean were reinforced during a three-month engagement in Malaysia where I taught lean through a simulation that a couple of Ernst & Young partners had developed using Lego blocks. By this point, I had travelled extensively for pleasure, but Malaysia, with its unique religious and political culture, placed me in a radically different situation: Not only was I in a Muslim country crowded with Chinese and Indian people (neither of whose cultures I had ever experienced), but I was consulting in a high tech plant. Although I had consulted in industries other than automotive, I had never done so where clean rooms and ångström-level tolerances were the norm. Cultural and environmental factors notwithstanding, lean still made sense to me — it applied just as readily there as in every other situation I had been in. Furthermore, the workers in Malaysia were more keen to apply their learnings than people I'd worked with in North America.

Eventually, this engagement led to a full-time job at Seagate (the company I was consulting for in Malaysia) as their lean subject matter expert. My crew there was impeccable, and everyone seemed to see lean exactly as I did. We had tremendous success all over the world with our projects. At one point, someone claimed that the lean benefit to Seagate in the first five years was in the order of $500M USD.

I was convinced that lean was something extremely valuable and that anyone who made the effort to understand it could reap its value. As a lean group at Seagate, we adopted many lean practices: Six Sigma techniques; ideas from just-in-time, total quality management, or the theory of constraints; and other associated methodologies. The practices (or tools) dovetailed so cleanly that they seemed to be a natural fit from the beginning. Lean was so simple, obvious, and natural that I never felt like I was teaching anyone anything. I was just helping them see lean's truth. Looking back, that simplicity was almost a spiritual experience for me.

Lean Literature Letdown

That all changed when I started my PhD in operations management. I began reading academic articles on this topic I knew so well. Dr. Robert Hall's *Zero Inventory* captured the mood of lean very well, and I found it very helpful. There was also *The Machine That Changed the World*, about the Toyota success, which I also found accurate and helpful. Both books were written by academics. Save those sources, no academic articles seemed to approach (and in fact many denied) the elegance and universality of lean that I had observed at Seagate. I was devastated that the literature (and by extension the great minds of operations management) captured so little of lean's benefit.

When I was looking for thesis topics, I mentioned that I would like to add to this operational literature with discussions around workplace culture. I was told that I would only have time to do that after I had received my PhD; until then, I should contribute something similar to what had already been published so that I would finish on time. You see, academia is in part a mutual admiration society, and since lean was not created by someone in that society (but rather by practitioners) it never got support consistent with the practitioner impact it had. Everyone was happy to steal the concept to show that it proved their hypothesis of performance improvement or supplier relations but they did not care whether they had represented it correctly. Recreating lean to make my name in academia would have been a long, ultimately futile slog given that so many people seemed ready to contort the concept for their own papers. With a heavy heart, I concluded that academia had failed the lean practitioner, and I withdrew from the program.

I tried to continue with lean but I found myself in the company of consultants who would sell isolated aspects of process improvement as if the aspects were their exclusive domain. More and more, when I looked at process-improvement resources, I saw articles written to promote individual consultants rather than clarify what lean is so that businesses could apply it on their own. This accessible concept that Taiichi Ohno had created at Toyota had been commandeered by academics on the one hand to write papers that do not help practitioners and repackaged by consultants on the other hand to drum up billable hours. I felt that both ways a business person was likely to learn more about process improvement — taking a course or hiring a consultant — were flawed. In light of this, I felt it was time to write a book, a do-it-yourself book for you, the decision maker, that included all the cultural nuances that were left out of the academic literature. I also wanted the book to shield you from consultants who sell simple solutions that offer no real long-term benefit. At Seagate, we always tried to train and consult so that when we walked away, the process improvement was sustainable and created follow-on successes. Sustainable and applied learning like that is what I hope to deliver in this book.

Why and How: Two Books in One

When talking about lean, there are two overlapping stories to be told: the *why* and the *how*. On the one hand, it is important to have the end in mind and to tie all decisions to that end. That is the *why* of lean — the philosophy and purpose of undertaking process improvement. Independently, there is also the story of what to do tomorrow, what to tell employees, and what to encourage or discourage. That is the *how* of lean — the tools and the concrete ways that you go about doing process improvement.

When working with business people, I find that they rightly want to know *both* the why and the how of process-improvement steps. When talking about a tool, I found it easy to get business people excited about how it worked, but I had to carefully explain why it was important so that they did not misuse the tool. And when I indicated the next stage of an improvement, as much as they understood why it fit the big picture, they would interrupt me to ask, "How do you do that?"

Flipping back and forth between the how and the why is simple in a face-to-face conversation, but in a book, where communication flows only from the author to the reader, such flipping can seem discontinuous. So, I address this concern by talking about the why in the main text and describing the how in sidebar discussions. I am, in fact, providing two books together so that you can conveniently switch back and forth at any point. Along the way, I will include anecdotes, training suggestions, and implementation notes to help you better understand the tools, which are completely interchangeable across process-improvement regimes as long as they are implemented with the right target in mind. It is beneficial for you to know these tools so that you feel comfortable deciding what to do in your process-improvement initiative.

This book addresses the stages of thinking that you should go through to make the best process-improvement decisions. First, I provide a primer on operations management because without a basic understanding of operations management, process improvement can be incorrectly seen as a salve. (Every company should have stabilized its operations management before making a decision on how to improve. Otherwise it would be like buying new tires to fix a problem with your car's axle.) Second, I help you detect and understand the process improvement that is already happening in your company, unbeknownst to you as a decision maker, and what that means for the company and the decision. Third, I discuss the decision as to which process-improvement regime would work best and how to set up the company for successful implementation.

The real benefit of this book is in the first two stages and how they empower the third stage, but it would not surprise me if readers jump to the third stage to find out how things end. I implore you not to skip to the end, as you will likely be unhappy with the results.

Chapter 2

An Overview of Lean

Lean Tools and Toolboxes

I have already referred to "tools" as the *how* of lean process improvement, and before proceeding further, I want to give you an overview of those tools and where they fit within the regimes known as Lean Manufacturing and Six Sigma.

It is essential to understand the major difference between Lean Manufacturing and Six Sigma. Lean aims to eliminate waste and ensure efficiency, while Six Sigma aims to eliminate defects and reduce variability. These different aims explain why lean focuses on the operator and Six Sigma focuses on the designer or engineer. But there's more. Six Sigma is a project-based, data-driven approach where statistical analysis is an important aspect of process improvement. It values cold, hard facts that require much of the project to be complete before a decision is made, as opposed to the intuition common in continuous improvement. Six Sigma uses two methodologies known by the acronyms DMAIC (Define, Measure, Analyze, Improve, Control) and IDOV (Identify, Design, Optimize, Verify); lean follows a more fluid PDCA (Plan, Do, Check, Act) methodology. Because Six Sigma requires more investment in a project-based approach and because it requires an understanding of statistics, it is not as accessible as lean or other regimes.

Here is a convenient summary of the regimes and their methodologies. At the back of the book, a chart lists some of the terminology used in the book.

Lean Is a Concept, Not a Cult

It always disturbs me to see lean principles made inaccessible to people by means of jargon and Japanese words. Apart from the odd time where there is no real translation, insisting on Japanese words is not necessary.

In the seminal book *The Machine That Changed the World*, the authors went to great lengths to argue that lean was not a direct function of Japanese culture and could have developed anywhere in the world. But in *Lean Thinking*, author James Womack (co-author of *The Machine That Changed the World*) changes his position and invests the Japanese words with magic. They are not!

Taiichi Onho, the father of lean, credits his inspiration to Henry Ford, who created the moving assembly line to speed up car production, helping each car get to the customer in a perfect form and in the shortest possible time. Ford's assembly line was completely consistent with the philosophy of lean, yet he did it all without studying in Japan and before the term "lean" had been coined. So why the need for Japanese words?

Jargon separates and excludes people much like the exclusive use of Latin in early universities. To belong to the cult of lean, you must learn the language, and you are rewarded by being recognized as one of the few! Both lean certification and Six Sigma belt designations further emphasize exclusivity. But lean works best when the person closest to the part is the one most involved in the improvement initiative. Some of the best projects I have seen in lean and Six Sigma have been proposed by people with no prior involvement in either regime. Making lean and Six Sigma approachable means more people can have educated input into your project.

In this book, I will occasionally use a Japanese term as a label for something, but my intention is to educate you about lean methodologies, not their Japanese names. I prefer to create a culture of lean through lean improvement stories rather than by promising exclusive membership.

I am also dubious about the various forms of lean certification. I assume that someone who is certified in lean manufacturing can run a quick improvement event and that someone who is a certified Six Sigma Black Belt can calculate the significance in a t-test, but beyond that, I'm not sure how certification contributes to competence, and I believe that recruiters who rely on certification are making a big mistake. In the current business climate where recruiters have to screen, they rely on certification to make the first cut. But certification, like a specific lean vocabulary, does not help process improvement. To properly assess the competence and suitability of job candidates, the incumbent manager should determine whether they can apply process-improvement tools in practice in a way that is suitable for the job.

When we taught lean at Seagate, we discussed how to grade our students and the consensus was that evaluation, no matter how rigorous, was less effective than having students demonstrate their knowledge on a project basis. So, students were responsible for three projects in areas related to the course content. As instructors, we validated whether a project used the right tools and whether it benefited Seagate, but beyond that, we did not evaluate students' performance. At their graduation ceremony when they received their certification, we displayed a summary of their projects behind them on an overhead projector. The ceremony was held in San Francisco every year, and their peers from around the world were present along with their boss and some executives, plus the COO and president of Seagate Technology. Having their peers and bosses recognize and appreciate their completed projects was the motivation for students to do well, not achieving a mark for knowing specific tools or terminology. The project orientation was very effective at getting students to study the techniques that made the most sense for their projects.

Simple But Not Easy

As a lean consultant and trainer, the most common thing I hear from the students at the end of a class or project is how simple the lean principles are. It is this simplicity that makes lean concepts so effective for process improvement. We have to promote this simplicity because it can open our eyes to what is possible beyond initial expectations. Moreover, any complexity in process-improvement tools tends to discourage involvement, and that in turn affects a project's outcome. Simplicity is best.

When teaching lean, I typically create models or simulations that immerse students in different situations. Unlike a lecture or case-style approach, simulations operate on many levels and allow students to experience the simplicity of lean. They can actively participate in their own learning and, regardless of their previous knowledge, usually find something worthwhile in the experience. But teaching Six Sigma is more challenging.

Six Sigma is statistical, and that can be a problem. The regime targets process designers and process engineers who ought to have a basic understanding of statistics, but the required statistical rigour is often beyond the capability of those who don't have scientific or engineering backgrounds. This isn't to say one should avoid Six Sigma in favour of lean or some other simpler process-improvement regime. Putting the process designer as the centre of the initiative still has benefits in many situations, but you have to weigh the advantages of using a tool like Six Sigma's statistical hypothesis testing against the costs, which include a lower rate of participation within the company. If, at the end of the day, you do decide to use Six Sigma tools, you will need to teach and support the statistical concepts.

Strategy (Why) Versus Tactics (How)

Focusing different process-improvement tools on a single level is desirable, but focusing on more than one level at a time could result in confusing goals for your organization.

Lean has long been known to focus on the front-line employee; when managers from General Motors toured Toyota, they were shocked to learn that front-line workers could stop the production line without management approval if or when they felt it was necessary. Alternatively, Six Sigma tends to focus on the engineering ranks and specifically the design and process engineers. The difference between focusing on front-line employees and the design and process engineers may seem subtle, but let me illustrate the conflict. Supposed you engage both front-line workers and engineers in a 5-whys exercise to get to the root of a problem. If the root cause is connected to a defective part from a supplier, the front-line response will begin with early identification of good and bad parts at the operator level. In contrast, the engineering response will be to redesign the product or process to eliminate the need for that part. Each is a positive step toward better and more stable processes, but they operate on different timelines and are somewhat mutually exclusive. Having front-line workers and engineers both attempting to fix the problem is redundant and misguided. To me, this is a clear example of where lean and Six Sigma differ and why Lean/Six Sigma is more a collection of tools than a proper philosophy.

Executing the Change — Change Roles

Earlier in this book, I explained that the philosophy and purpose of a process-improvement initiative represents the *why* of things, whereas what to do tomorrow, what to tell employees, and what to encourage or discourage represent the tools and practices or *how* of things. I consider *why* questions to be strategic and *how* questions to be tactical. I have also given you an overview of the different tools and practices and explained that specific ones in Appendix 2, while interchangeable, need to be directed at the people who have the most impact on the customer benefit.

One of the least understood truisms of change management is that corporate cultures can only migrate from what they used to do to what they should be doing one project at a time. It is easy to dismiss this after the change has occurred but during the change there were projects led by change agents whose success or failure created the culture that currently exists. There are three key people involved in any good transition: the leader or visionary, the change agent, and the initiative manager. On occasion, one person will be the change agent and the initiative manager, but they are distinct roles.

Leader/Visionary

Someone in management has to condone a given project on a business level or the project will fail from lack of support. Ideally, the leader or visionary will create a vision for what has to happen and then all projects will be coordinated to close that gap. In every other situation (where the leader is at best complicit), the change will have limited scope and likely take the company in disparate directions. Nonetheless, there has to be someone in management who remains in a role of managing the business (not the change) and who will lead, resource, and validate the change. If they try to do double duty and be change agent as well, they will no longer be recognized as putting the business before the change and they will be seen as part of the project and not objectively part of the business. For the most part the leader or visionary will act as a steering committee for the change.

Change Agent

Independent of the leader/visionary, someone on the ground will be piloting the change in a tactical way. This involves making hundreds of decisions such as what size, what colour, for how long, and with what people. This person has to know the tools to employ and how to use them to reach the outcomes laid out by the leader/visionary. If the "why" part of the book is for the leader/visionary, the "how" part of the book is for the change agent.

Initiative Manager

For the first few projects, you will not need anyone managing the initiative, just as for one or two projects you will not need a project-management office. However, once expectations have been set based on a few successful projects, you will need to coordinate the projects going forward to live up to those expectations and continue the push. The initiative manager has three responsibilities: 1. Create a process to mine for new projects; 2. Inform current change agents of past projects that were similar to theirs for purposes of efficiency and consistency; and 3. Archive complete projects in such a way that they are retrievable and useful for ongoing projects.

This role in current process improvement is obscure and less understood. As well, this role is often filled collectively by giving current change agents the responsibility to research and archive their projects. However, as much as the roles of change agent and initiative manager do not have to be exclusive, they are different. Having a single point of contact (even if they share time with other change agent duties) is important to the infrastructure of the initiative.

Mining for New Projects

Once people start to see the benefit of process improvement, it tends to splinter. As much as people see the intended benefits and try to duplicate those benefits, others will promote the ancillary good and selfishly try to make that a bigger part of the change. For example, whenever I have been a part of a successful 5S implementation, other managers will line up hoping to get their areas "cleaned up" as well — not recognizing that a clean work area is a consequence of 5S and not the purpose. There has to be a way to collect all new project ideas, vet them for utility, and organize them as to importance and priority. If not, valuable resources will be squandered on pet projects that go nowhere and teach nothing.

It is common to have a hopper of good projects waiting for resources to come available. Quite often I have stored these in a two-dimensional matrix with them rated on value on one axis and ease of implementation on the other. This approach is my most effective way of getting the most value out of new projects based on the resources that come available.

In the event that the hopper dries up (people stop suggesting projects), the initiative manager can go back to the leader/ visionary and have a brainstorming session (usually including change agents) on what is next in executing the vision. This often takes the form of a Value-Stream-map review or a metrics update.

Supporting Current Projects and Archiving Completed Projects

As much as these two activities are separate, they come from the same infrastructure. The primary decision in this infrastructure is "What project metrics are important?" This goes back to why you started the project (reduce inventory, control variability, and one-piece-flow flexibility) and who you want to target as the resource that has the most impact on customer satisfaction. If you are tracking too many metrics in your archiving of projects, it's a sign that you do not have a clear vision as to where you're going. Plant metrics may seem unrelated to project mining and project archiving at first but you quickly realize that it is the only thing worth researching! I see this coordination of vision, plant metrics, and target resources as the specific philosophy of your particular process improvement.

The Problem with Conflicting Philosophies

The tools you use for process improvement should be applied based on the same philosophy. If you don't pay attention to this or have an ambiguous philosophy, you will likely create confusion and tension in the implementation. For example, you may have trouble if you simultaneously do activity-based costing and theory of constraints because they may conflict on a philosophical level. Let me illustrate.

Some colleagues of mine consulted with an apparel man-ufacturer that had just completed an activity-based costing (ABC) analysis. According to the ABC analysis, the compa-ny should not sell white T-shirts because the cost of the pro-portioned activities exceed the contribution made from sell-ing them. However, the theory of constraints analysis that was done later indicated that the thread-dye machine was the bottleneck. Given that white T-shirts are not affected by the thread-dye machine, one could argue that it does not cost any-thing to manufacture the white T-shirts (materials aside) be-cause all overhead costs should be applied to the bottleneck. So, the philosophies underlying these tools clearly contradict each other in this instance: If you believe that the factory is limited by the output of the bottleneck, you should sell as many white T-shirts as you can, provided you do not affect the bottleneck. On the other hand, if you believe that the activities applied to processes are variable and distinct, you should not sell any white T-shirts.

Lean Manufacturing Versus Six Sigma?

When I worked at Seagate, we had two problems. 1. Smooth new-product introduction was the most lucrative side of our business, and we recognized that the involvement of engineers would reduce variability and better track the voice of the customer. This concern lent itself well to Six Sigma. 2. At the same time, our product (the computer hard-disk drive) was becoming a commodity, so we had to do more with less. Doing more with less required just-in-time supply in our supply chains and better control of front-line operations to eliminate error. This situation lent itself well to lean. In response to this dilemma, Seagate chose to have a corporate-sponsored Six Sigma organization but there was also a grassroots Lean Manufacturing group that came in at pretty much the same time. (I was in effect a founding member of the latter.) In as much as we could cherry-pick our areas of improvement, the Lean Manufacturing and Six Sigma groups were each very successful.

However, when each group got bigger, there was a push from on high to merge the groups in order to reduce overlap. This push had the unintended effect of having each group articulate what it represented and making that more important than what the other initiative represented. In those discussions (of which I was a part), it became very clear that there were trade-offs that the groups themselves were not in a position to decide. Everyone agreed that all the tools should be taught to both groups and that there were ways to merge lean into a Define-Measure-Analyze-Improve-Control structure. However, when it came to reporting metrics (production or quality based) and how to prioritize projects, it was clear to the lean group that the engineers were going to win given the high-tech environment.

I have been to Lean/Six Sigma conferences where a large percentage of the time was spent on the difficulties of merging Lean Manufacturing and Six Sigma groups. Nobody ever disputes that the tools can be shared, so merging the groups seems obvious, but there are always people in the discussion with horror stories about the integration. The people with those stories always ask, "If it makes so much sense to merge Lean Manufacturing and Six Sigma groups, then why didn't it work for me?"

When Seagate merged its Lean Manufacturing and Six Sigma groups, it became clear that product introduction was more important than daily operations, and the new Lean/Six Sigma group bore that out in metrics and project prioritization. In your implementation, you may not have to decide between Lean Manufacturing or Six Sigma (or even Lean/Six Sigma), but you will have to identify and articulate what is important to you so that all of your effort can be focused on improving it. Once you have decided on your focus, then you can call the initiative whatever you want.

Chapter 3

The Basics of Operations Management

A friend of mine was looking for help with his company and he wanted me to tell him whether he should do Lean Manufacturing or Six Sigma. No, I gently told him. His company was neither ready for Lean Manufacturing nor Six Sigma, as it suffered from basic scheduling, inventory, and organizational issues. As hard as that was to tell him, saying anything else would have caused more harm than good. What his company needed was effective operations management, the subject of this chapter.

Before you decide to do any form of process improvement, your company needs to have stable operations, meaning that
- output is regular and predictable;
- quality issues are infrequent and obvious;
- inventory levels are properly understood and surprise stock shortages are infrequent; and
- the bottleneck is known, and everyone agrees on the path and what the difficulties of increasing the capacity beyond that are.

In other words, you have to understand and apply what's known as operations management.

Why Operations Management?

Operations management is the study of things in business that take time. One may argue that everything in business takes time, so operations management is about everything in business.

This is technically true, but for practical purposes in operations management, activities are ignored if time is not involved. Accounting, for instance, is not an operations management concern because accountants focus on how money movement is tracked, not the time involved in tracking it. However, at tax season, the amount of time it takes to prepare a tax return for a client may be significant enough to be of concern to operations management. So, to be more precise, operations management is the study of things in business that take time when the time element matters.

A chapter on operations management may seem odd in a book on process improvement, as if I am suggesting that minutia must be considered as part of a high-level decision. I don't expect that readers look forward to a discussion of operations management when they are likely reading this book to decide between Lean Manufacturing and Six Sigma. But here is the thing: I have seen way too many companies with weak operations management adopt process improvement as a way to get good at operations management. It doesn't work that way. In fact, a poor foundation in operations management is more likely to contaminate their process-improvement effort.

Doing process improvement without having effective operations management is a lot like hiring an Olympic swimming coach and then admitting that you don't know how to swim. You need to have a foundation in all aspects of business, especially your operations, or you will be entrenching as many bad practices as you will fix.

When I worked at General Motors in the 1990s, ISO 9000 (and the automotive version, QS 9000) was all the rage. ISO 9000 is a process-capture system that forces companies to document everything done in operations. To be fair, it helped a lot of companies without any systems in place for their operations because it forced them to decide what they did in operations. However, ISO 9000 became an impediment to those businesses later because as they and their market changed, some of their systems also had to change. Companies that relied on ISO 9000 as their only approach found it difficult to rationalize and manage change over time. As much as ISO 9000 gave them some operational stability, it would have been much easier (and cheaper) to fix the operations-management piece independent of the ISO 9000 implementation.

Process Improvement No Substitute

In some sense, the popularity of lean (and other process-improvement regimes) stems from its ability to reintroduce general operations management principles. Newer lean tools such as Value-Stream mapping speak to firms that do not have stable operations. (In this case, you should not have to send people to Value-Stream-mapping training if they already know how to map processes.) However, using process improvement as a tool to fix the missing knowledge can only offer short-term gains. The real solution is to identify the missing knowledge and find a way to acquire it. In this regard, lean has the benefit of creating manufacturing knowledge by improving local know-how about the situation and the details at hand and teaching most implementers an enormous amount about operations management. However, what quickly becomes clear is that not all of this know-how is transferable, and some issues get "solved" over and over again because the root cause was never addressed. In short, lean cannot replace a broader understanding of operations management.

To be clear, this book is not meant to instruct on how or why to elevate the discipline of operations management (even though that should be important). Rather, this book (and specifically this chapter) will help you identify and remedy any current gaps in your operations management knowledge.

Companies that do not practice proper operations management may not recognize their operational issues. After all, they likely have an operations management department (even if under a different name) so when they implement some tools it should be made clear how much improvement was the impact of the tool as opposed to the halo effect of improving their operations management. Likewise, my experience as a consultant is that inferior operations-management departments will occasionally feel threatened by process improvement that goes beyond their knowledge and try to sabotage the effort.

The first step in every process-improvement effort should be verifying that you have the right operations-management people in place. As much as process improvement can work anywhere, some tactical decisions needed during implementation can only come from people who understand and will continue to promote your operations strategy. The nature of globalization has changed the regional views of operations management, so even if you are paying your operations management staff exorbitant amounts of money, they may not be versed in everything you need. For reasons that I will explain later in this chapter, there is a shortage of good operations managers at this time.

Operations Management Comes First

As a general rule, a company's operations are not easy to understand or assimilate. When I take students on plant tours, they comment most on how much it takes to control all of the different inputs that go into operations, and when we simulate factory operations with Lego blocks or folded paper, they have difficulty interpreting the experience. They have trouble identifying what tasks or metrics are important in all of the noise. And students who are assigned to "manage" our simulated factories — even those with day jobs in operations — cannot say how much they would expect to produce in a given period; their answers tend to be unrealistically low or unrealistically high. All this is meant to convey that the common person (and sometimes the common operations manager) has a limited understanding of what is going on in the business operations and how to manage it. This holds true in even the simplest of operations.

This dearth of operations understanding is a big problem in process improvement given that the best implementations occur when there is candid input from many people who understand the operations. Over and above making high-level operations decisions, the operations manager must make operations transparent so that process improvement can come from the people closest to the problem (often not the operations manager). (You need to understand that operations opacity or obfuscation is often the sophistry of insecure operations managers.) Whether out of need or by coincidence, the first successful process-improvement projects are often associated with creating a better understanding of the operational situation or stabilizing it. It is imperative to all process-improvement initiatives that operations are made clear to everyone involved. Clarity makes the operations easier to manage (by anyone including the operations manager) and allows for more constructive input from those who are not managers.

Before you start any process improvement, your operations management should be able to do the following:

- map your process;

- identify key process steps (bottleneck identification);

- involve stakeholders from different departments in the decisions;

- represent internal and external customers in decisions;

- articulate what consistent behaviours are required to produce customer-acceptable quality; and

- associate tasks and actions with company strategy.

Furthermore, before deciding on a process-improvement regime at the corporate level (notwithstanding some early stabilization or green-belt projects), operations should also be able to do the following:

- identify the bottleneck for all typical production situations;

- reasonably and representatively predict production outcomes; and

- calculate the manufacturing cycle time (the time required for a representative part to go from raw material to saleable good in the current process).

If you cannot do this, your effort is better spent directly fixing your operations management group.

To further make this point, the following table of Lean Manufacturing/Six Sigma tools will be redundant if your company already practises sound operations management. These tools should only be used for emphasis, because appropriate activities should be taking place in your operations long before any process improvement is done.

Lean Tools That Seem Redundant to Basic Operations Management

Lean Tool	Operations should already be
Going to the Gemba	Frequently observing and interacting with operators
Value-Stream Mapping	Process mapping and documenting process modifications
Cross-functional Teams	Involving stakeholders in decisions
Hoshin Kanri	Adopting clear management objectives based on strategic discussions
Voice of Customer (Six Sigma)	Representing the needs of both internal and external customers in decisions

If your operations departments do not already do the things in the right column, using the tools in the left column will not only be unproductive but will likely solidify any current bad habits in your operations.

Beware of delegating functions to a consultant that should properly be done by your own operations people. I heard of one advertising consulting company who will send consultants to your store to observe your customers. They just watch what people pick up off the shelf, what they look at on the label, and what they eventually decide to buy. It seems brilliant to be able to think of such a simple approach: These consultants are touted as brilliant outliers. But my question is, "When did store managers stop doing that?" In the Six Sigma regime, there is a discussion of the voice of the customer. I was shocked to learn that this somehow seemed new and needed its own section, but apparently in today's business climate it does.

The Demise of Operations Management

During the 20th century, North American companies had world renown for their ability to manage operations. In fact, Henry Ford and Frederick Taylor led the world in process management. North

America also led the way academically in operations organization (Sloan and his introduction of divisions in corporations) and quality (from the likes of W. Edwards Deming, Joseph Juran, and Philip Crosby). However, North America's days as the paragon of manufacturing have expired. There is less and less focus on operations management — in manufacturing, specifically, and in services, by extension. I lament this not because I think that operations management is the only business dimension worth recognizing, but rather because I think it is a discipline that we once had and have now lost. The U.S. is known for Silicon Valley innovation, creative finance, and disruptive technology overall. The U.S. is and likely will continue to be the world's biggest economy as these great business investments reap benefits. That notwithstanding, North Americans think they still have manufacturing dominance. They don't.

North America (and by extension most rich countries) have experienced a tremendous amount of offshoring — the relocation of operations from one country to another — in the last few decades. This is primarily because of the differential between factory costs (mostly labour) in local and offshore markets and the cost of the transportation of goods in lieu of local manufacturing. Some products, like gravel, are bulky enough and have so little value-added labour content that they may never be produced offshore. However, as global infrastructure improves (as it has in the last two decades), the cost of transportation goes down and the propensity to relocate established industries offshore increases.

The decision to relocate operations to another country is typically made on the basis of labour costs, but production and sales decisions are more dependent on capital costs. For any company, the limit to what they can produce and sell is a function of only one culprit, the "bottleneck," that point of congestion in your operations that creates delays and limits capacity. In some cases, the bottleneck is external. For instance, supply is limited or demand is less than what could be supplied. But quite often, the bottleneck is a function of an internal resource like a machine or worker. In manufacturing, the bottleneck often ends up being a machine and, in most cases, the most expensive machine.

A bottleneck can often be found because of an iterative back-and-forth between operations, and capital purchasing resists expansion when the cost of a new machine is too high. For example, if I am an automotive supplier with an assembly line, the line will account for a large portion of the cost of the plant. If I could produce more output by simply buying a parts washer for $100,000, I would not likely meet with too much resistance to add this capacity. But if I propose specialty equipment that costs just under $1,000,000, I will likely get an initial rejection until eventually the need justifies the cost. The tendency is to resist capital expenditures. If the only way to produce more is to build a second assembly line, the push will be to gain efficiency on the existing assembly line to avoid the cost of building a new one. For this reason, most assembly plants' production is limited by the speed of their assembly line.

However, if automotive and other capital-intensive industries move manufacturing overseas, there is arguably less need to focus on using what the company has in an efficient manner because most arrangements work on a variable cost structure and reducing those costs is seen as a negotiation outcome, not an equipment-utilization outcome. Consequently, businesses that produce offshore focus more on logistics than on production or quality. When logistics plays an outsized role, we lose whatever knowledge advantage we had in operations management, as well as our ability to develop new knowledge to deal with current manufacturing issues. This seems unimportant only if you assume that we no longer manufacture anything domestically. In fact, we still manufacture a lot, but those doing the manufacturing are ignored as if they are on their way offshore.

Some people claim that North America still maintains superiority in design, but that assumes that design and manufacturing are not linked, when they really are. There are two modes of design — design based on manufacturing insight and design based on market insight. Given that China is the fastest-growing market in the world and that its manufacturing is growing, I suspect that we have already lost any design superiority to them.

Anecdotal evidence shows that operations management departments in North American universities have shrunk or have been merged with other disciplines, evincing its lower status. Most educational institutions offering business degrees have moved to "global business" or "international business" degrees, implying that there is no need to produce anything domestically and thus no need to study production management. Operations management of products and services in North America has atrophied into a rump that is the study of logistics.

The shortsightedness of this narrowing of focus in business education is clear. First, there is no mechanism to shift the focus back to recognition of a need for a broader understanding of operations management. New businesses that produce locally do not know what they are missing. Second, because our understanding of services management stems from an understanding of operations management, even our understanding of how to deliver services is negatively affected. So, this narrow view of operations management will continue unabated until a crisis in manufacturing (or services) competitiveness is confronted. (A good example of what to expect in such a situation would be what was experienced in automotive manufacturing in the 1990s when the big three North American automakers were overwhelmed by Japanese auto manufacturers and only later scrambled to recover some of what had been lost.)

Operations Management — Anybody Home?

As much as offshoring and other distractions have taken the focus away from operations management, your organization may lack proper operations management simply because it was never put in place. I recently consulted at a small factory where the owner wanted me to help the supervisor get better at knowing what to purchase in a timely manner. The owner had a dedicated whiteboard for listing needed purchases. However, there was no urgency indicated for any item, and after the products were purchased, there was no mechanism to remove items from the list. Clearly, no one could trust the whiteboard, so the supervisor resorted to text messaging the owner to indicate what was needed, as well as posting items on the whiteboard. The owner complained that texts arrived too late and reached him after he had already visited the associated vendor. Anyone with knowledge of purchasing will see this example as a recipe for frequent, costly, and often unnecessary purchases. But the owner swore by it. When I dug a little deeper, I realized that purchased inputs were stored haphazardly to the point where it was hard to understand what items were available. When I tried to create organization for the storage of purchased items to assist in inventory control and purchase efficiency, the owner said that my suggestion had already been tried and failed, so there was no sense in retrying.

One could argue that this problem lends itself nicely to a 5S project — sort, straighten, shine, standardize, and sustain — because one possible solution is having everything in its place, and a 5S project should improve process flow and consistency. However, to do justice to a 5S project, you have to define and limit its scope. In the case of this factory, if we were to limit the scope to prime production, we would not capture ancillary items like light bulbs and toilet paper, which were ordered the same way as production inputs. On the other hand, if we were to include all purchases, the project would become intractable because it would have to include what-ifs that could not be exhaustively counted.

The proper solution for the factory is to classify items as either high-volume movers (A items), sporadic or seasonal movers (B items), and items whose volume or value is so low that they're not worth a lot of attention (C items). Only A items require a dedicated spot on the shelves. B items will have some dedicated spots but will likely change in some patterns based on seasons, and C items get whatever space is left. Without this analysis, a 5S project provides no advantage. And without either, there is very little in the way of operational control of purchasing.

This is just one example of many where operations-management systems (such as organized inventory and purchasing prioritization) are absent. I have also consulted with many service companies where decision makers feel that operations principles don't apply because there is no "product." Having taught services management at the university level, I can attest that service organizations need operations management just as much as manufacturers do, albeit in different ways. Services often lack a product to follow, but it is still important (often even more so) to capture the flow of information and demand signals that relate to the service being delivered. A process map, flow chart, Gantt chart, service blueprint, or some form of flow capture must be a regular part of the operations-management process. Otherwise, attempts to do Value-Stream mapping as part of process improvement will be wasted on fundamental questions rather than clarifications. Without some sort of predictable and identifiable operations process, a process improvement will devolve to "Try to do better than yesterday."

Visualizing Your Existing Process

The first step in any operational project is to understand the process. Both Value-Stream mapping and process mapping are tools that allow you to visually identify how your process works today so you can determine what is and is not currently working and identify what you want to preserve or improve in your business. A process map is a high-level picture of a process within defined boundaries. A Value-Stream map is an enhanced process map that focuses on materials and information and includes data about timing.

When teaching operations management at the introductory level, one of the first things I always do is introduce the process view of operations and discuss process mapping. If you cannot create a process map, you are the operations-management equivalent of illiterate. I am not saying you have to keep process maps on file and up to date (though this is required for some certifications in the food industry), but your level of familiarity with process maps should not be in the range of "I made one once." So, I assume that every operations department has some skill in process mapping. Even so, I am baffled by the popularity of Value-Stream mapping, which I think of as process mapping with the inclusion of a few specified variables.

I once heard a story about how Value-Stream mapping started. The story is that when the first few Value-Stream maps were found at Toyota, the people there dismissed them. Apparently, however, the North Americans who were just learning about lean concluded that the maps, with their specific metrics around cycle time and inventory, were Toyota's way to track lean progress, even though the people from Toyota never mentioned the maps as part of the Toyota Production System (which was the template for lean). It took North Americans to "discover" and promote Value-Stream mapping as something special. I have to think that the people at Toyota had a good laugh at the North Americans making a big deal of one of the most basic operations management tools ever known. However, that does not stop consultants from making money from the repackaging of basic operations understanding.

I thought the fervour around Value-Stream mapping would die off, but it hasn't. I still see plenty of job descriptions where knowledge and experience with it is a requirement. Presenters at lean conferences include tremendous detail on their Value-Stream maps, yet all one can ever prove is that you know the process (which as I stated before should be the base assumption). I have taught Value-Stream mapping, but only to highlight its lean metrics and that it obliges the project manager to consider process impact. It does not warrant the attention it is getting.

If your operations people are not familiar with process mapping, a comprehensive course on Value-Stream mapping will teach them process mapping. However, if they do not understand process mapping, there may be a whole lot they do not know.

Make sure that everyone in the lean organization (and all operations people in your factory) knows how to map processes. It is fundamental to pro forma planning in operations. Then, once you get to Value-Stream mapping, the discussion can focus on why the lean metrics are highlighted and how they roll up to macro indicators such as manufacturing cycle time and first-time-through quality.

The Number You Care About Most

It's easy to collect data and to manipulate that data in various ways, but how do you know what matters and what doesn't? Before you embark on a process-improvement initiative, you need to establish a single metric, the one number you care about and want to focus on and improve upon.

One of the appeals of process improvement is that you get to view your operations through a single lens. This simplicity is helpful in communicating gains, comparing potential projects and developing momentum. The concept of lean is about reducing waste, and as long as you choose an appropriate metric to reduce waste (inventory levels, manufacturing cycle time, response time, etc.) you are on the right path. At Seagate, it took more than 100 days to go from raw material to a finished hard drive, and in my tenure there, we reduced the number of days in that cycle from 100 to the low 90s, returning significant savings to the company in the form of inventory and customer response. When I worked with the Six Sigma group at Seagate, the focus was on z-score, a statistical concept that we used to calculate the probability of getting every product right. These are examples of the kinds of numbers that we cared about most at Seagate at that time. When I start consulting projects or have job interviews, I typically ask the person on the other side of the desk what metrics matter most to them. If they seem confused by the question or if they answer in terms of a financial metric (like EBITDA) then I worry that they have not gone through the exercise of knowing what operationally is important to them.

In general, you will always be able to come up with a number you care about most because every reason for starting process improvement contains something measurable. In your process improvement, a single metric will help you clarify (notwithstanding some checks and balances) and manage an otherwise unruly task. That having been said, it is important that you feel comfortable choosing what metric you want to excel at and determining what to do when gains are less than beneficial.

As an example of the need to focus, let me walk you through a common situation in process improvement. Let's say I am brought in as a consultant to reduce manufacturing cycle time. Thus I can tell everyone involved that manufacturing cycle time is the key metric. You will still have to observe other metrics to effectively run operations but the domain of the improvement is specific. But if you ask someone on your process-improvement team what the focus of their project is and they reply something inconsistent with manufacturing cycle time (like head count), you have a problem. Taking it further, you may be able to reduce manufacturing cycle time and as a consequence also reduce the labour hours required. At that point the question of what to do with the extra bodies comes up. Management usually takes the position that they should be retrenched but this could completely reverse the benefits gained in manufacturing cycle time. I then find myself in a debate with management where they ask how they can justify paying people they don't need and I have to counter with the fact that the company is now doing more than before with fewer people and thereby registering tremendous cost savings. The company is way ahead even if they pay the people to play cards. However, trying to gain additional (and proportionally less) labour savings may sour the mood and put an end to any process-improvement effort. To be fair, I can often recommend productive projects for the idle labour to take on, but the issue still is that the focus changes from one metric to another and thereby messes everything up. How the metrics get rolled up to a corporate level, how the projects get chosen, and how the projects are resourced should all depend on a single corporate goal based on why the process-improvement project was implemented!

The Uses and Abuses of Numbers

Metrics are valuable, but care must be taken. Numbers can be used *and* abused, and the more specific the number, the more care is required when putting it to use.

Recently, I heard that recruiters spend on average six seconds per resume. I am not talking about an isolated case, but a statement regarding how the world of recruiting has evolved. In this amount of time, a recruiter is restricted to only one or two metrics they can assess (other than a cursory check for a key word or line). From what I have heard, they justify the short assessment because they typically receive more than a hundred resumes for any posting. They likely support that justification with the observation that only a few metrics matter at any one point. Let me dispute these justifications separately.

If we accept that a large workload justifies substandard work, we are simply accepting substandard work. If a professional wine taster only spent six seconds reviewing a wine, we would not pay any attention to his review. Vetting candidates that work in our companies must be more important than rating a wine. Teaching at the university level, I have students who feel overwhelmed by the reading I assign; they come to class having only skimmed it and they typically pay the price by not doing well in my class. In any situation, shirking responsibility for not doing the work well because there is so much volume constitutes failure.

It is true that only a few metrics matter at any one point. (In fact, one of my favourite operations mantras is "not everything matters.") However, a recruiter needs to read the resumes to find out what does matter! And only then can the recruiter determine what part doesn't matter. Assuming that you can specify what material does not matter before you have even read it implies that you are looking for something exceedingly specific. Filling a hole may be what everyone thinks they need in recruiting, but that is the job of a mechanic, not a manager. People are not interchangeable and work cultures change over time. Seemingly disparate points on a resume such as volunteer time, travel, approaches to work, and tasks accomplished matter more than a single metric such as "years in the field" or certifications. I once talked to a manager at a bank who was recruiting a process-improvement position. He told me that he read each of the one hundred or so resumes that he received, and he was then chided by his human resources department for doing so much work. This is clearly the type of person I would like to work for (notwithstanding the misguided human resources department).

In a similar vein, management dashboards — at-a-glance progress reports — of updated metrics have become all the rage. Managers are happy to have one place to look at to see all of the key metrics. I am all for centralizing key metrics, but not to the point that we think they are the only metrics. The world cannot be contained in the domain of a few variables. Even the metrics on the dashboard (if they are any good) speak to matters with more depth than numbers can convey.

I teach a class on statistical process control (SPC) where we use a type of chart known as an Xbar-R chart to examine whether a process is in control. The students can usually get their head around the math and the charting. However, their responses vary according to what the chart indicates. If the chart indicates things are in control, they are happy, but if the chart indicates things are not in control, they seem confused. I explain that when the chart indicates things are not in control, it does not necessarily mean that there is a defect. Instead, it means that you have to go to the process and see what is going on. They seem stuck on this notion that the chart should tell *how* the process is not in control, even though I tell them that there is no way of knowing which of the thousands of ways the process is not in control unless you go see the process for yourself.

Getting firsthand knowledge of any process is proper operations management. Don't let people convince you that it is the new best thing.

To Hire Right, Know Your Operations

Knowing your process includes knowing what employees do at each stage of the process and the key traits for each job. There are three possibilities for screening applicants in hiring: Staff can be screened and rewarded for their ability to 1. follow the rules (obedience), 2. apply good judgment (judgment), or 3. put people at ease (behaviour). Consider a triangle with these positive traits being the vertices. You will never be able to focus on all three because some people who have great judgment may not be very good with people. For example, you may excuse a doctor's poor bedside manner if he or she is exceptional at judging the pathology based on the symptoms. (Remember the TV show *House*?) With some effort, you can identify which traits are most important in which amounts and that specification will afford efficiency in your screening process. It is wasteful to screen for a sub-optimal trait where another trait is more important. An in-depth understanding of how your staff fit into your operations is essential if you want to hire wisely.

Establishing a Quality Baseline

Lean Manufacturing and Six Sigma are often considered part of the quality movement, so it would be fair to assume that adopting either or both will improve quality. However, as with general operations, a baseline of quality should be present before you adopt any process-improvement initiative. This baseline has two components: 1. knowing what quality is for your customer (i.e., knowing how your customers define quality), and 2. having some system to predict and record your current conformance (how well your product or service meets your standards for quality).

A company has to do a lot of things to establish quality for what it sells, and it is incumbent upon a company to maintain customer expectations once those have been established. However, making good on the promise to customers falls on more than operations management because quality is less about operations than it is about the company's strategic offerings and how customers measure and define quality. It is really the customer and the company strategy that creates expectations about quality, and understanding the role of operations in meeting those expectations is key to understanding quality in operations.

I say that quality is defined by the customer, but that can seem glib. Let me illustrate. I once consulted with a small retail grocery operation where the owner was trying to show me how hard it was for him to buy the right produce for his customers because the banana representative offered seven different grades of banana. The owner wanted to attract a higher-value clientele, so he was considering stocking a higher grade of banana, but was daunted by seven different grades. I replied that his customers only considered two grades of bananas: yellow, which they would buy, and brown, which they would not buy. As a store owner, he should stock the cheapest grade (or combination of grades) that will give the customers yellow bananas every time they come in.

It is daft for management (and specifically operations) to chase higher quality without recognizing how the customer will receive it. Customers will signal or confirm what they want, and it is up to operations to supply it as consistently and cheaply as possible. It is not up to operations to offer better — *that* is a strategic decision — and operations should be chided for doing any more than is expected if additional resources are required. So back to the banana example: Buying a grade of banana that is yellow for three days and a second grade that is yellow for seven days to cover the seven days between orders makes sense, but buying higher-grade bananas to blindly impress customers is a waste of money.

For customers, some aspects of quality are absolutely necessary before they will purchase something. I call these "must-haves." Other aspects of quality are desirable options that customers will pay more for. I call these "value-adds." We can represent these components of the buying decision with concentric circles — the smallest circle having a list of must-have's and the outer circle having the value-adds. As an illustration, consider me buying a coffee on my way to work:

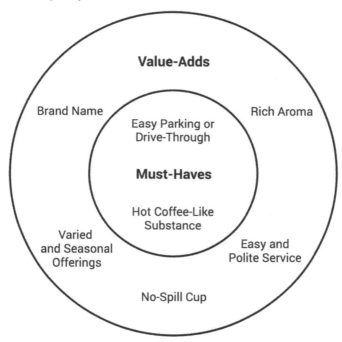

I am looking for convenience, so I will reject any place with a long line or cumbersome parking. At the bare minimum, I want a place that sells some kind of hot coffee in a way that does not cause me a lot of grief. I only need one parking spot or one drive-through lane, so places with many available parking spots or multiple drive-through lanes are not any better in my eyes. Once I have dismissed places that cannot provide my must-haves, I can then focus on value-adds.

I typically respond to brand (as the taste and aroma of different brands do create some brand memory), and I might be tempted by a new flavour or seasonal offering as well as a no-spill cup. Also, I may see a place where I remember having received exceptionally polite service, so I may put more consideration on that location or even pay a premium to go there. Not everyone will have the same profile as me, but if you can find groups of customers who have similar profiles, you could market to that group more effectively by having a summary profile that represents them.

You will notice that very few of the aspects mentioned in the circles directly involve operations. If the lines for buying coffee get too long, this would suggest that operations may be taking too long to fulfill orders, but otherwise operations input is limited to brewing the right amount of coffee so that it is fresh and hot, and serving it with a smile. The spill-proof cup and aroma aren't the responsibility of operations and usually fall within the purview of sourcing as directed by marketing input.

Occasionally, you will hear about people in operations who will try to affect quality by putting more time or effort into a process. Their effort should be rewarded in as much as it affects conformance (how well their output meets the expectation of customers). However, their effort is not a good way to change customers' expectation of quality for the better.

In his talks, Tom Peters used to discuss people in companies who went above and beyond expectations and (in his view) shattered customer expectations. I remember his story of an employee at Federal Express (a delivery service) who took the initiative to rent a helicopter to personally ensure that deliveries got through. The presentation seemed to imply that the company has people who are capable of changing quality expectations — but this is wrong. After having heard the story, I do not have any higher expectations from my local Federal Express office than what is stated in the service contract. And the hero of the story is not disrupting the market in the quality dimension as much as conforming to the existing expectations of getting the deliveries through on time. To suggest that this radical employee is changing the quality the company offers is to misunderstand how operations management affects quality. If the company wants to capitalize on this tale, it can reset quality expectations through marketing, but it should not be forced into it by the single act of a line employee instead of by a thorough understanding of the segments they serve.

In any event, the first role of operations around quality is to establish the quality expectations of the customer. From there they can connect the quality model to the company strategy and find some way to measure it. Operations management is only responsible for the measurement. When it comes down to it, operations' job is to get the quality "good enough" as quickly, cheaply and consistently as possible.

Managing Operations — Parts Flow and Bottlenecks

You have to consider two perspectives when managing operations. The first is the perspective of the part that flows through the operation. It is incumbent on a manager (and, ultimately, the person facilitating a process-improvement initiative) to follow the flow of the part in real time. In practical terms, that means "stapling" yourself to the part and following it through the process. You do that less to see where it goes (as a mapping exercise) and more to see what decisions are made in the process and why. Typically, with this exercise you will find that parts wait in unsuspecting places for less-than-obvious reasons, and the priorities of operators are not always consistent with standard protocol. These observations (as well as path deviations and rework loops) provide great insight to anyone trying to improve the process.

In the case of service industries, the "part" is people (often the customer). For example, in a restaurant you may be forgiven for thinking that the meal is the main product, but any restaurateur knows that the customer is sold on everything *but* the meal. So, following a hungry customer through the process of becoming a satisfied customer will often create insight as to why customer complaints happen.

The second perspective to consider when managing operations is the bottleneck. The bottleneck is the constraint in the process: the one part of the process that, if given more resources, would allow the process to be more productive. People often incorrectly think that output is maximized by giving every process more resources. In reality, only one operation is the bottleneck at any given time, and identifying that bottleneck and managing it becomes important to process improvement.

In your operations, you need to be able to identify and diagnose your company's bottlenecks. Some bottlenecks are temporary and will move if there is a change in the production schedule or staffing. These are often quickly fixed with minor process improvements and better operational visibility. Enduring bottlenecks, on the other hand, tend to exist where capital equipment is expensive or the process takes special skill or judgment. In other instances, the bottleneck is external and there is more than enough capacity in the operation. When the constraint is external to your company, you should direct your efforts to how to sell more or improve supply, instead of studying the bottleneck.

When touring an automotive plant with students, I am often asked if I know where the bottleneck is. I do, and finding it is a lot simpler than students think. The bottleneck is the assembly line and/or paint line that snakes through prime real estate. The capacity of these lines is often dictated by hardware rather than the number of people supporting it. So, if an automotive plant wanted to grow, it could do a whole bunch of relatively cheap things before putting in an exorbitant amount of money to build a new assembly line or paint line.

In the case of a dentist's office or mail room you would hope that the dentist or the mail processing is the bottleneck or you have to ask what went wrong. If the receptionist at the dentist's office is working so slowly that the dentist has to wait, you have an easier fix than needing to hire another dentist.

In taking a bottleneck perspective, you have to plant yourself at the bottleneck and capture in note form everything that happens insofar as time is concerned. A good approach is a time study in which you survey the bottleneck and ask questions that relate to an instant in time. Your notes will help you find ways to get more output from the bottleneck or at least determine what resources are holding you back.

I recently did such an analysis of an engineering department that I thought was a bottleneck. The first question to ask is whether the machine (or in this case, engineer) is working. If the machine is working, a simple note as such is usually sufficient. There may be some situations where the machine or operation is unusually slow, but for the purpose of such a study, if it is working then that is fine. If it is not working, I write down what the machine or operation is waiting for. In process improvement, you want more output and, thus, more quality time from the bottleneck, so what you write down becomes the basis of improvement.

Often people will forget that the time study should be from the bottleneck's perspective. Instead, they make notes about the operator manning the bottleneck. For example, they might note that the machine was down because the operator had to go to the bathroom. The bottleneck time is important — the operator time may not be. So, if another operator was available while the first operator was in the bathroom, the issue is staffing (not biology or the proximity of washrooms). However, if the bottleneck is the dentist, it is appropriate to note that because an absent dentist means lost production.

Once you have good information about how often and when the bottleneck doesn't do what it is intended to do, you can apply the theory of constraints. The theory of constraints is illuminated in *The Goal* by Eli Goldratt and Jeff Cox — a simple, recommended read for anyone in operations. *The Goal* identifies five steps to improve the output of the bottleneck (or "constraint" in the language of the book).

The bottleneck affects the output of the entire process, so the first area to look for process improvement is in the bottleneck's own backyard. Going beyond this can disrupt the operation and other improvement efforts, so hold off changing other areas until you have exhausted opportunities at the bottleneck itself. In some cases, improvements can be made there through improved scheduling that prioritizes certain inputs, by better staffing arrangements, or by simple capture and annunciation of downtime.

Once you have done what you can within the operation to improve it (and as long as the operation is still the bottleneck), you should look at shared resources that are applied to the bottleneck — collective staffing, ancillary support, management attention, etc. — and prioritize those resources. This can be disruptive for the process overall, but is important as long as it improves overall output. Furthermore, you should consider moving testing that would normally happen downstream of the bottleneck to just before the bottleneck to ensure that the bottleneck is only working on good inputs. Part of the consideration at this stage should be breaking down the operation to decide which aspects are best routinized (or even automated) and which are the domain of skilled operators to eliminate mismatches in staffing or resourcing. As well, part hand-off in the operation should be scrutinized so that the bottleneck is doing the least part manipulation possible. Up until now, no additional resources have been added necessarily. Current resources have just been manipulated to increase the capacity at the bottleneck.

If the bottleneck persists once you have prioritized shared resources in its favour, the next step is to increase capacity through newly acquired resources. This step is even more disruptive than the previous two and often has an impact on the organizational culture; it should be attempted only when the previous two steps have been exhausted. However, at this point you typically are dealing with an enduring bottleneck and applying serious process improvement is not only valuable but often the only way to make production headway. Upper management is often involved at this stage and it is important that decisions are consistent with the corporate strategy and improve the corporate culture. As much as the suggestions are coming from workers closest to the operation, the true decisions now rest with upper management.

There are an infinite number of ways to increase the capacity of a bottleneck if you have infinite resources, but the increase in output must justify the cost of new resources. This involves a thorough discussion of economies and diseconomies of scale for your process. Once you have fully addressed economies of scale and optimal resourcing, the bottleneck becomes stable and predictable, notwithstanding drastic changes in the competitive environment.

Chapter 4

Assessing Readiness for Process Improvement

Certain conditions need to be in place before you can responsibly decide which process-improvement regime and tools you are going to adopt. In the last chapter, I described the first of these conditions: You have to have stable operations. In this chapter, I describe the second condition: You need a change-ready culture. That condition is essential if you want to make improvements that get your product or service to your customer in a perfect form and in the shortest possible time. It doesn't matter whether your company produces tangible goods, offers services, or facilitates banking and commercial transactions.

In order to assess your company's readiness for change, you must intimately understand the operator's role in process improvement, something this chapter will teach you. With that understanding, you can identify and support improvements that may already be taking place informally at the operator's level, and you can select appropriate tools from the lean toolbox to encourage process improvement in a more formal way. This chapter also details some of the tools in the lean toolbox that apply at the operator level.

There are two potential ways to start a process-improvement program in a company. 1. Upper management can concede idea generation to the appropriate employees and use management power to support them as change agents; or 2. Self-identified change agents can work in areas that management doesn't contest. Of the two, the Machiavellian approach of willfully avoiding confronting the change agent is the most common but it can only go on for so long before management is effectively sanctioning all informal change initiatives. Management needs to be the gatekeeper for ideas to make sure that they align with the corporate strategy, but management still has the herculean task of empowering the workers to come up with the ideas.

Ready for What?

It should be clear by now that a decision to proceed with a process-improvement effort is not trivial. Your improvement effort must correspond with your strategic intentions as well as with your available resources. Committing the company to a process-improvement plan is expensive in terms of the dollars you will invest and the human capital you will allocate. Yet, in most cases, the decision is based on the recommendation of a consultant who knows very little about the corporation and its culture. This book tries to clarify the weaknesses of such recommendations and to prepare you for the overarching decision of the corporate direction as well as associated decisions about project tracking, project metrics, and project idea generation. The most important point is that the best decision does not come from the boardroom or the CEO's office, where it is typically made. It comes from the day-to-day operations of the business.

The concept of lean is based on the philosophy that a product should get to the customer in a perfect form and in the shortest possible time, hindered only by our ability to create barriers and defects. This philosophy is sound and really does apply everywhere — in manufacturing as well as service industries.

Lean Manufacturing is sometimes described as the elimination of the seven wastes: transport, inventory, motion, waiting, overprocessing, overproduction, and defects. An eighth waste, unused human resources, was later added in the book *Lean Thinking*. Six Sigma, with its emphasis on statistics, focuses on eliminating or minimizing all variability. The theory of constraints focuses on maximizing the throughput of the bottleneck. But all of these process-improvement approaches contribute to the notion of getting the product or service to the customer in a perfect form in the shortest possible time. Following that philosophy will allow you to lower inventory costs (in my experience usually by half), reduce defects, and improve responsiveness to the point where companies who do lean well are a disruptive force in their industry (witness Toyota against GM, Ford, and Chrysler).

But I'm getting ahead of myself. Before you embark on any process-improvement initiative, you need to have a change-ready culture, which exists when

- performance metrics are simple and have a direct connection to company success; and
- there are common, recent examples of successful projects.

If either of these is missing, you have work to do before you commit to a process-improvement regime.

The ultimate success of process improvement rests on your employees having the will to make the changes and the relevant know-how. Many programs fail because too few people are engaged at the grassroots level. A litmus test for your company's change readiness is a root-cause analysis where people discuss a defect and then brainstorm what could account for such a defect. You ask why a defect occurred and then ask "why" for every subsequent answer until you arrive at what you can identify as the root cause. If employees present only obvious, evasive answers in this exercise, you are not ready to start process improvements on a corporate scale.

In addition to assessing the amount and quality of grassroots involvement, you have to gauge how your management will react to a suggestion because they have the first opportunity to squash any improvement effort. Process improvement is an emergent process and cannot be dictated from on high. For some managers, giving up that control can be unsettling, and the reluctance to do so may explain why suggestion programs adopted by North American automotive companies never reached the success achieved by Toyota — too many good ideas were struck down by management.

Ideally, early improvement projects come from the people who are doing the work. If you are not getting good projects, employees may not be ready or management may be squashing their efforts. Management efforts to feed employees potentially good projects should be discouraged, as they will lead to top-down failure. The effort has to come from the bottom!

The best lean implementations always start with an operator who has the insight and motivation to improve their operation. This often happens long before management decides on or even recognizes the need for process improvement. In other process-improvement regimes, someone in a position to make a difference identifies and coordinates an improvement effort, but my experience shows that lean improvements, meaning those occurring at the operator level, are the most recognizable and easiest to get going. Most process-improvement regimes try to stoke this motivation after the initiative has been launched by creating quick-wins or small projects around low-hanging fruit. However, the adoption runs a lot smoother when there is already evidence that improvement was occurring locally on an informal or spontaneous basis.

Supporting Early Initiatives

Changing a corporate culture is hard. When you unilaterally decide that your company is going to adopt a process-improvement regime without properly assessing the environment, your workers will resist your efforts. But if you pay attention and take care, you may find that process improvement is already taking place on an informal, local level. This becomes the ideal foundation on which to build your corporate initiative. When an operator suggests how to improve the process that will cost little more than their time, managers are typically more than happy to accommodate the improvement. In the manager's day, full of chasing laggards, compensating for ill-suited management policies, and executing piles of administrative work, they will likely relish a diversion with a positive purpose. So, giving some employee with progressive views assistance seems easy to justify. To be fair, any request that includes a significant capital budget will get shot down, but if a kernel of a good idea is recognized, even this type of offering is welcomed with some advice to find a cheaper way.

And this is typically how lean starts — with operator initiative. Often, the projects involve something very simple like moving a storage location or identifying a way to get a faster response. Nonetheless, any win (no matter how small) will be celebrated, and the operator will now be emboldened to try larger projects.

In general, you should encourage this kind of informal, local change, but you do need to be able to assess the quality of operator-driven initiatives. For the project to be a good project, it must do one of two things:

- Bring clarity to operations in some way; and
- Have a very focused measurable outcome.

Most people think that both of these criteria are needed for a project to have value, and true, projects that meet both criteria would be most valuable. However, in the early stages of process improvement, it is beneficial to allow many new "lean practitioners" to start projects as long as they truly believe in them. If you foresee an improvement in the clarity of the operations or a marked improvement in a key metric such as cycle time or first-time yield, then it is worth endorsing the project. In assessing any particular initiative, consider the benefit of the project, the benefit of enabling a new lean practitioner, and the buzz around a small win.

That notwithstanding, middle managers should be wary of sending too much capital to any of these early projects. Project owners should get intrinsic satisfaction from executing their projects, and if they somehow get special treatment (big budgets, extended time off, special tooling, etc.), others may be tempted to start projects for the wrong reasons.

The focus should be on small projects related to the operator's set of decisions. Resist the temptation to implement any of the following at this early stage, as none of them will be helpful.

- increased pay
- longer breaks
- employee training (of a general nature)
- change in target customer
- anything not specific to the operator and their interaction to the specific process

All of those suggestions can be justified later on at a strategic level, once the process has been stabilized and made obvious. The primary purpose at this stage is for the operator to make decisions about how they can help the part get to the customer faster and in a defect-free way, and the secondary purpose is to make the process easier for everyone to understand.

In lean circles, there is a saying that the first suggestion is the most expensive. The saying may not be entirely true, but the point is that if you look closer you will likely find a cheaper (and often better) way to carry out an improvement than the one initially suggested. A litmus test for these types of projects is that you should push back if the project requires any approval from outside the department. There are usually enough cheap and easy projects that you will not need to go outside the department early on. Once the majority of projects come in with payback longer than a year, it is time to move to a coordination system aligned with your company strategy.

Early lean projects are often so small in scope that they seem insignificant and thus are ignored by upper management. This is good! Ironically, it is lack of significance that allows the projects to bypass the middle-management resistance and bureaucracy that can plague corporate-wide improvement initiatives. Moreover, until some significant successful outcomes can be identified that warrant debate and the accompanying political heat, it is counter-productive to publically recognize informal champions of process improvement. Giving them the spotlight too early tends to either flood a process-improvement initiative with undue resistance or open the door to political meddling. As a manager, the best you can do is allow informal champions to decide what makes the most sense given the way *they* see the problem. It is not up to the manager to change the project in any way but rather, as best they can, to remove barriers that could stall the project. Typically, these early projects are small enough that they do not burden front-line management. Allowing local initiatives to be small and keeping them under the radar (and thus immune from management meddling) is important.

But beware of suggestions to change layout. Minor layout changes may be acceptable, but invariably the operator will want to change the layout more than is really necessary.

I run a simulation where participants learn process improvement by taking on the roles of operators in a factory that makes simple structures from Lego blocks. At the end of the initial production run, I ask the operators what we could do to improve their processes. Many of the suggestions are quite helpful and fall within the areas where operators can legitimately make improvements. However, invariably someone suggests changing the layout of the plant, even though a layout change benefits no individual directly and provides indirect benefits through better communication, visibility, and logistics. In addition to providing limited benefits, a layout change tends to be exceptionally costly in real life once you consider everything that it involves, namely,

- the physical costs of moving equipment as well as disassembly/reassembly, requalification, and start-up issues;

- the cost of lost production while the move takes place as well as disruption to other processes that are nearby;

- the need to gain consensus among many players who may represent disparate positions based on the benefits they see. So even before anything is moved there may be some labour hours lost in discussions and animosity related to differing views of the improvement; and

- the ephemeral nature of the benefits. The change, once made, produces new interactions among operators or processes, which in turn generate ideas for further layout changes that may undo the original change. Thus, the situation escalates, and the (misunderstood) justification for the original change somehow justifies a new investment, creating a cycle where the number of changes increases without corresponding benefits. This invariably erodes the credibility of those who endorsed the change. One might argue that the cascade of layout changes is progressive and necessary, but given the costs involved, such change should not be started until the larger organization has bought into the process-improvement initiative.

Layout changes often serve as a panacea because no one is directly accountable for the benefits or the costs, given the number of people involved. Nor do the changes target the good or bad output of any one person. The anonymity that makes a layout change so appealing is the very reason why it is unhelpful at this stage of process improvement.

What Operators Have to Contribute

As much as we would like to believe operators understand the big picture, the unit of analysis for the operator is the part of the process they affect and not the macro process. This is a fact, not a problem. You need to be aware of the operator's scope so you have a realistic picture of their role in process improvement and be able to spot informal improvements that operators make on their own initiative.

Where Project Ideas Come From

In my experience, if you give workers the means, they will find valuable improvement projects to carry out. Workers usually come up with their own disparate projects if left to their own devices but at some point there is a need to come up with good follow-on projects and coordinate all projects to some common goals. As much as I want to specify the kinds of projects you should promote and where to start looking for them, project identification is not the domain of management. When it first introduced Lean Manufacturing, Toyota had a program to encourage suggestions from employees, and that program was a big driver of project ideas. GM, Ford, and Chrysler didn't empower employees this way because they had different thoughts about who should drive change. In my opinion, no matter what process improvement you choose, implementation should focus on the people who are coming up with project ideas that get the best product to the customer the fastest. By allowing those people to see what is possible, you are taking your first step towards successful process improvement.

There is a finite number of areas where an operator can improve a process. In particular, the operator can
- validate the inbound inputs;
- clarify/validate the schedule to be certain what inputs need to be affected and how;
- qualify the input as a good one before it is processed;
- process the inputs efficiently;
- orient the inbound inputs so that they are easy to process;

- create an environment so that everything required for the process is visible and ready for use;
- set up the environment to process a specific input at the expense of other inputs;
- simplify/streamline the steps to process the input;
- determine that the output meets required standards as soon as possible after processing;
- get the environment ready to efficiently process the next input (by clearing or resetting the station);
- advance the input or output;
- clear the finished input or output to ready it for the next step in an efficient way (does not impede production of subsequent inputs); and
- let downstream players know that the operator's process is complete.

In early projects, it would not make sense for an operator to improve all or even more than one of these areas, but typically they can affect at least one of them.

It is important to recognize that these operator improvement areas are not exclusive to manufacturing but apply to repetitive service work as well. So, we could as easily consider the above analysis to relate to a garment being sewn in a high-volume production area, a garment being sewn in a repair shop, or even the design of a garment (no physical content) going through a design approval process. As long as the process is established within certain parameters, the input need not be physical. However, the analysis would not apply to random processes such as a doctor responding to a patient, where the number of possible ways to respond is theoretically unbounded. Rather, this model is limited to processes where the operator's possible responses fall within an obvious range, whether the process involves a tangible product, a service, or a transaction.

Educating and Engaging Employees

Some companies try to encourage process improvement and engage employees by explicitly asking for suggestions, but this does not necessarily contribute to a change-ready workplace. In fact, if not handled properly, suggestion programs can generate resistance and resentment. When I worked at General Motors, the company set up a suggestion program to save money, and every suggestion was graded on the net dollar savings. At first blush, it is hard to find fault with this approach. The problem was that most operators did not know which activities made money and which did not, so their suggestions were not necessarily in the best interests of the company. Initially, a lot of suggestions involved eliminating a part or eliminating a process or some material substitution that would obviously save money, but they were not necessarily conducive to selling cars. So, many suggestions that met the published criteria of saving money were rejected. The suggestion program lost credibility because workers chafed at what seemed like capricious responses to thoughtful suggestions and, eventually, it became a place for employees to vent. To address the cynicism, management would occasionally reward some of the better (albeit potentially unusable) suggestions, but that did not change the attitude that employees developed towards the program. I was not privy to the costs and benefits of the suggestion program, but I have a hard time believing that any cost saving attributable to employee suggestions outweighed the monetary and workplace costs associated with the program.

Companies that open up their books and educate workers about the costs associated with company business tend to have better suggestion programs. Customers are not necessarily served better if accountants run your machines but sharing basic accounting information with employees broadens their horizons and helps them understand where they fit in the overall company picture.

When I was at Seagate, I don't know that there was any official suggestion program, but in all of the lean classes, we taught that the throughput time to get a part from raw material to customer was a key metric. And the Six Sigma side of the house explained the importance of first-time-through yield or z-score so students knew what to suggest. Teaching operators or designers more about the time it takes to make the product or alerting them to yield issues was completely in line with Seagate's strategy of getting the product to the market first and without defect. If there had been a suggestion program at Seagate based on either manufacturing cycle time or z-score, the corporate responses would have come across as a lot less capricious than the ones at General Motors, because Seagate employees understood how their work related to the overall corporate strategy. At Seagate, suggestions were discussed and assessed in a holistic way, on the basis of corporate strategy instead of on cost alone. Having said that, there is something satisfying about quoting dollar savings, so even at Seagate we were not immune to the temptation of dollar discussions. When management became critical of the process-improvement efforts it was often associated with a period of declared cost savings without an associated strategic benefit.

For process improvement to succeed, you have to explain your company's strategy in a way the workers can understand and relate to. But employee engagement is a two-way street: While employees need to understand the company's strategy and see where their particular process fits into the overall picture, the company also needs to appreciate the employee's vantage point and what actually goes on in the workplace. To this end, as a consultant the most valuable thing I can do at the start of a process-improvement project is staple myself to an order and follow it through the process. In lean we call this "going to the Gemba," which means going to where the work is actually done. By following an order in real time, we can identify key points where the order waits, gets diverted, misprocessed, or any number of things apart from getting to the customer in the fastest way and in the best condition. Management often resists going to where the work is done — in some instances because the conditions on the work floor are dirty, hectic, loud, unsafe, or boring. In other instances, the resistance is based on the belief that a monitoring system gives all necessary information, without the need for managers to go to the work floor. None of these excuses should deter you from going to where you can see, feel, hear, smell, and touch the work area for yourself.

At Seagate, a lot of the production happened in a clean room, which required everyone gowning before going in and de-gowning when they were done. I still found the exercise valuable every time I went in and well worth the effort of gowning and having my vision and hearing obstructed by the clean-room attire. There is no substitute for being there. The workers are typically there every day, but if you are going to be of any help as management or as a process-improvement facilitator you have to be there with them.

Operator Improvement 1 — Validating Inbound Inputs

The operator only benefits the corporation and the customer if they work on the right inputs. For instance, if a pizza maker applies the wrong or mouldy cheese to a pizza, the customer will not want the pizza. If a bank teller sends funds to the wrong account, the customer's money won't get where it's intended to go, and the misdirection could cause more problems. In both cases, the operator is doing the right thing (making a pizza or transferring money to an account) but the inputs (type of cheese or destination account identifier) are wrong. Unless the right inputs (physical or information) are applied in both manufacturing and service businesses, the outputs are defective.

Inputs that are obviously defective or wrong can be avoided or eliminated by checking, as long as the check is cheap and unambiguous. Checks that create cost or require new decisions (explicit or implicit) should only be considered later, when the whole organization has bought in to the process-improvement initiative. Introducing them earlier than that usually causes more problems than benefits.

Consider the process of tossing a can into a recycle bin. A cover on a receptacle that is in the shape of a can is clear and unambiguous; the shape obviously matches a pop can and not a newspaper or other recyclable product. The receptacle cover with a hole shaped for a can is also fairly low cost. In contrast, a sign saying "This receptacle is only for recyclable products" is ambiguous because there is no commonly accepted definition for recyclable products. This type of passive inspection is ideal for process inputs.

When the wrong inputs have been applied, the typical response is to add another check in the form of an additional inspection, but even if the new inspection is cheap and unambiguous, it is almost always counterproductive and creates more problems than it solves. As long as inspectors know that there is another inspection to rely upon (either upstream or downstream), they feel absolved of responsibility. For example, having the teller "double-check" the identifier for the destination account sounds

Lean Tool: Error Proofing or Poka-Yoke

Error proofing can greatly minimizes defects (although errors may or may not lead to defects), but, ironically, that is not its primary value. Eliminating an error has value over and above a statistical improvement on defects. The real goal of error proofing is the process predictability and stability it affords.

Let me offer an illustration: Consider a bowl of salt on a table in a coffee shop and its potential to introduce an error. Someone could easily think the bowl contained sugar and inadvertently put salt in their coffee, thus completely ruining the taste. Now let's say your goal is to make sure you always have a perfect-tasting cup of coffee. To achieve this goal, the benefit of labelling the salt or removing it from the environment is undisputed. However, it does not even show up on the radar of someone who is focused on the perfect cup of coffee. Fixing the error of misidentifying salt as sugar does not in itself make much difference to the taste and quality of the coffee. You are better off investing in better equipment and better coffee beans. That said, eliminating the salt error makes the process of making a perfect cup of coffee more stable and contributes to other coffee improvement efforts.

Some people see error proofing as "defect proofing." But this is overly optimistic. Although error proofing can minimize defects, the opportunity for defects exceeds our ability to error proof in any realistic sense. So those who think that defect proofing is possible and that error proofing is the way to achieve it will likely be disappointed with error proofing and may deride it as useless. It is not. In fact, if your expectation is that error proofing will help stabilize your process and set you up better to address defects in a plan-do-check-act or statistical way, it is invaluable.

Error proofing implies you have an error (not a defect) and you can eliminate it in a binary (not statistical) sense. Statistically, there is an ever-present (albeit diminishing) probability of a defect based on specific mechanisms in the operations. Error proofing is not about changing these statistics as much as changing the mechanism so that the variability is gone. It is unrealistic to do this to the entire operation, but there are some errors that can be *completely* eliminated this way.

like a way to avoid input errors, but typically the teller either rechecks the same source (which may be flawed in the first place) or asks the client to repeat the information, which takes more of the customer's time, creating cost. Furthermore, once there is an external process to validate the account identifier, the teller has little incentive to get it right in the first place because "they check that again later, anyway."

For a new check to be effective, it should ensure good output from the process step and only apply locally to that specific step. At an early stage, it is best to focus directly and unambiguously on one process step and one operator at a time.

Operator Improvement 2 — Processing Inputs Efficiently

Typically, lean efforts begin with projects like 5S, a way of organizing the workplace, and visual factory, a way of reducing waste. Often, these projects are small and go unrecognized because their implementation is so simple. However, having operators work through these projects is beneficial on many levels:

• In implementations run by operators, the operator learns more about the operation through tinkering with it and is empowered to continue improvements.

• Even though the operator leads the change in their own area, the operator often confers with others, allowing for multiple views and multiple considerations. This improves the outcome of the change and strengthens the operator's status and confidence as a leader.

• Changes made typically create clarity about the operation so that others can better understand the operations and provide better input to the change initiative.

• Other operators notice the activity and consider improvements in their own areas.

I have commonly seen all four benefits recognized in projects where operators are left to their own devices with no pressing timeline. However, the middle two benefits tend to disappear or get curtailed when the projects get rushed, if indeed they are

Fishbone Diagram

The fishbone diagram (or Ishikawa Diagram, named after its originator, Kaoru Ishikawa) is a simple yet effective tool to brainstorm all of the errors that could contribute to a specific defect. The premise is that we can start with a defect (the head of the fish) and categorically associate errors that contribute to that defect (branch bones). The typical approach is to label the main branches as People, Process, Equipment, Management, Environment, and Materials. Given that the fishbone diagram is a brainstorming tool, the specific categories for the branch bones are not very important as long as they are 1. meaningful for the participants of the brainstorming exercise and those who will use the results; 2. collectively representative of the entire area for which you want to brainstorm; and 3. distinct enough that there is no ambiguity about where entries should be attached. Again, there is an important distinction between defect and error that the fishbone diagram bridges. There is no guarantee that you will (or can) capture all possible errors and thus you will never have a diagram that eliminates all defects. However, common defects tend to follow patterns and the fishbone diagram helps us understand how these patterns may be formed.

There is nothing magical about the commonly used branch bone titles except that they are mutually exclusive and collectively exhaustive. I say that, but invariably you will have someone entering an error that involves the operator using the wrong tool in the branches labelled "equipment," "environment" and "people" (and "training" if it is included). This would indicate that the inputs to the tool use may not be as mutually exclusive as our arbitrary categorization. Thankfully this hiccup will not stop the brainstorming process from producing some good insights.

In services, the customer often has as much impact on the transaction as any other input so you will want to represent the customer foibles somewhere in the diagram as well. This is not to say that through this process we can "correct" or eliminate the customer (there are, in fact, some approaches where we can eliminate the customer or their impact, but that decision should rest with the strategists and not the operations people). However, we can identify what customer behaviours are detrimental to the process, and in this way, we can understand errors in how we inform the projects, a word that implies a recognized end point. Calling the change a project often creates unnecessary urgency or detrimental political maneuvering.

In the early stage of lean, operators should be allowed to tinker with projects as long as they feel they can improve them. Creating time limits often limits the project's benefits. From a management level, projects are required for accounting and coordination across project areas, but management intervention tends to stifle *continuous* improvement. As long as the project is small (in resources and complexity, at least) and does not need to be dovetailed into other projects, the operator should be given as much time as needed and allowed to revisit the project as often as needed.

Projects also lose value when the manager (or anyone else) tries to change the project in a direction that the operator is not comfortable with. For maximum success, it is important that 1. The operator retain final decision making; 2. the manager's role is limited to clearing barriers so that the operator can make the right decisions; and 3. others support the operator through honest feedback based on direct observation.

Operator Improvement 3 — Advancing Outputs

When inputs have been processed, they typically move on to another part of the operation and make way for the next input. Under a pull scenario, annunciation — the use of signalling or notification devices — is one way to move outputs efficiently along in a process, and it often makes sense in an automated scenario whether the operator or a downstream agent retrieves the output.

One of the biggest changes I have seen over the decades in automotive factories is the application of Andon lights (that signal the status of an automated machine) to help the operators manage banks of automated machines at a glance. It would be hard to imagine operators having to physically approach each machine to establish what the machine was doing, yet when I worked at General Motors a quarter of a century ago, that was the way manufacturing was done. Having some indicator annunciate customer of what is happening or what they should do — much like how we would look at communication errors with employees.

Understanding the error is what we are trying to accomplish. We typically have an anecdotal idea of what the error is but the fishbone diagram allows us to discuss, validate, and define the error.

To see how the fishbone diagram can be helpful, consider the defect of locking your keys in the car (see page 61).

The general categories of "people," "environment," and "equipment" are represented in this diagram, but they are changed slightly to match the situation. To begin filling in your diagram, you want to consider the recent failure modes and what errors you feel contributed to them. As the discussion ensues, other potential errors will come to mind and you should include them. For each branch you should include a primary cause of the defect in terms of an error; from there, you can add branches off the primary branch that capture secondary causes, tertiary causes, and so on until you feel you have captured all the root causes. For misplaced keys it is hard to branch off too many times before you find redundancy among the "twigs" of the different branches, but if you are looking at complex products like cars or planes you will likely be able to go well past the primary cause to branches of branches of branches...

You will see some patterns emerging in the diagram. Some will represent biases of the participants and often it takes a strong facilitator to bring the discussion back to objective views. For example, if many of the causes have an uncanny link to budgets or a particular scapegoat, you will want to keep going and adding branches to see if the bias endures or if something more representative emerges.

If you get enough entries from open discussions, you will likely see representative patterns emerging that will lead to a potential area of focus for error proofing. In the above situation, routines and the ability to locate keys seem to be two culprits for errors. We next want to identify which errors represent binary decisions (should I close or lock the door) and which do not (I wanted to close the door slightly to clear room for another car but I must have pushed it too hard and it closed). Only the binary decisions are the domain of error proofing. There is still a lot of work to be done (and specifics of the car and driver to be considered), but we can start to identify error proofing techniques.

to the operator or material handler that the part or output is ready often makes plenty of sense.

Usually, it is the operator who moves the output along and hands it off, but sometimes, a different person or entity — a material handler, downstream operator, or customer — clears the processed input, in which case the operator should think about how changes in the operation impact those others downstream. It is far too common for process-improvement projects to improve one aspect of a process but inadvertently cause more problems. So, even though early process-improvement projects focus on one operation and the decision making rests with the operator, they should be tasked with ensuring that they do not create more problems in the processes up- or downstream. This can easily be facilitated by requiring the operator to notice the customer (or other entity) and their concerns.

To understand the practicalities of hand off, consider the express checkout in a grocery store. The express lane is unique because it addresses the needs of customers with fewer products to be purchased and thus fewer scans to be performed. Implicit in the line is the promise of speed; the express line ought to go faster than lines not designated as express. When I shop, I usually have few items, so carrying them to the checkout and to my car would normally be quite easy. However, after I pay the checkout attendant, they will hand me the receipt for the transaction pressed against the change that I am owed. This configuration makes sense for the attendant who can make the change from the till, quickly grab the receipt with the same hand, and give everything to me at once. From their standpoint, they are affecting the transaction as quickly as possible and thus creating the best situation for processing the line quickly. This doesn't work well for me, the customer, however. I have three different storage locations: one each for paper money, coins, and receipts, and I require two hands to sort what I am given. Paper money goes in the centre section of my wallet, which I keep in my pocket. Receipts also go in my wallet, but they need to be folded and tucked into a separate section. Coins are stored in a separate change purse that I carry in a different pocket. Given that my hands are already occupied with my groceries because the express lane has few areas to put anything down,

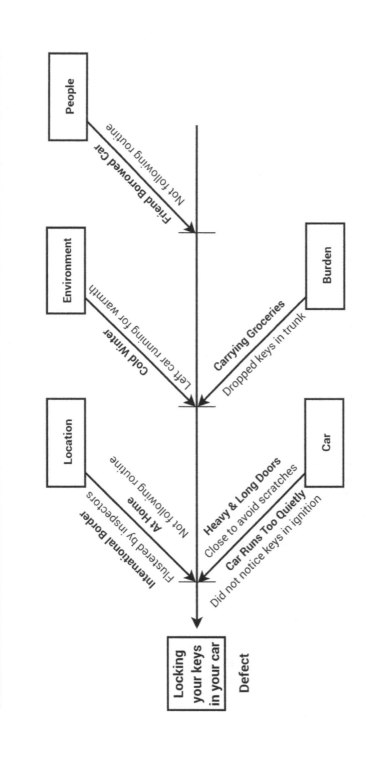

I am further slowed by trying to manage what is already in my hands. This slows my egress and thus reduces the number of customers the attendant can serve.

Given that new customers who are waiting in line cannot be served until the current customer is processed effectively, a better approach should be considered. Considering the transfer method that best helps the customer clear the checkout lane may be best for everyone even if it takes a little more effort or time on the part of the checkout attendant. Everyone wins if customers can be processed faster.

As things stand, the net effect of the attendant's efficiency is to create inefficiency in the customers' process so that, ultimately, the store does not realize any of the benefits that it intended or assumed for its express checkout. Furthermore, the attendant is likely causing the customer anxiety, having essentially moved the bottleneck from their processing of customers to the customer's handling of their output.

If you want an operation to go faster, focusing on hand-offs (of parts or information) is usually a good place to start. Were my change to be sorted and handed to me separately as coins, bills, and receipts, I might be able to deal with all of it with one hand and not have to create such a delay. However, the attendant is so enamoured with the "efficiency" that they cannot see that they have made the process worse and created anxiety for the most important person in the process — the customer.

Orientation matters in how quickly and readily an operator can perform their next task. In some cases, the physical orientation matters, such as whether the part is presented to the operator upside down or facing the right way. In my express checkout example, a different orientation for the output (coins, then bills, then the receipt) would facilitate a faster exit for me and improve the efficiency of the checkout process for me and others. Of course, there are subtleties of orientation that matter such as which side up, which hand receives it, assistance for heavy or awkward parts, and so forth. Getting this right is not the most important part of the project (it is often skipped when inexperienced project managers are at the helm), but there are sound reasons to take orientation into considerations. The best systematic way to capture any inconsistencies is to schedule a

For example, consider the binary error of misplacing the key in the car when the door is locked. In our initial brainstorming, we might start generating some error proofing solutions. For example, key sensors are one way to determine if the keys are either inside or outside the car; that might be useful. We might need more information to solve the error of "not following the routine," but it makes sense that we might start with thinking about positive routines we could foster and how to eliminate deviation from that routine.

I would likely start by thinking about key location. This would lead to 5S type solutions, where there is a place for the keys when they are not in the car (a special hook or saucer) and a place for the keys when they are in the car but not in the ignition (a place ideally visible from outside the car). This course of action will not eliminate the defect of locking the keys in the car, but it might help us eliminate the error of leaving the keys in some arbitrary place.

A couple more notes on fishbone diagrams:

Keep a copy. For many error proofing projects, I like to keep a copy of the fishbone diagram in the project files. It is surprising how seemingly unrelated defects inform healthy root-cause discussions. As well, I find new project managers will throw anything unrelated at a fishbone diagram just to say it was done. Only when I tell them that I want to keep a copy do they go back and add relevant items to it (and unwittingly get the insights they should have gotten the first time).

Use pencil and paper. I have seen many consultants peddle software solutions to avoid pencil and paper fishbone diagrams, but there is no need to go digital. First of all, this information is not so valuable that I need a digitally editable copy — a snapshot works just fine. Also, no matter what scale you choose, you will always have valuable bits of information squeezed into some corner of the fishbone diagram that would otherwise be lost in an electronic version. A fishbone diagram is and should always be a paper exercise. Even if you redo the exact same project a year down the road, you are better off working from an electronic photograph of the first fishbone diagram and creating a new paper version to represent the new reality than starting from an electronic template that you have used before. The power of the exercise comes from putting pencil to paper, rather than any insight borrowed from the past.

test run where you can experiment and solicit feedback from the customer.

In some cases, an input is presented to operators but it has to be preprocessed before it can be used. A modern example that comes to mind is when I buy an apple. Giving an apple a quick wash before eating it has always made sense, but as of late, grocery stores put stickers on apples. Now, before I eat my apple, I have to remove the sticker as well as wash it. The sticker also has to be discarded, so the process is complicated with an additional processing step as well as the need to dispose of waste. It doesn't take much time to remove a fruit sticker, but it does take time and effort to find a waste bin. There is an advantage to using apples that do not have stickers!

Orientation issues are not as obvious in settings where information is communicated, but they are worth considering because process improvements can be made at the operator level there, too. It is easier to analyze the transfer of physical products, but analyzing information transfers is often time well spent.

Every company I go into has reports penned for "someone else" in the company. Unfortunately, the majority of these reports capture information efficiently for an operator but not necessarily for the benefit of the end user. To see how bad this problem is (and to help fix it), display the different reports in a boardroom and have the end users indicate with a sticker or department name which reports they use. One of your first realizations might be that not all the reports have an end user. (You would be shocked at how many reports are obsolete and should be discontinued. Finding these is more valuable than the time you invest in setting up the exercise.) Then, have end users highlight what information they need reported and how they use it. This will tell you whether the report communicates key information efficiently and effectively. When I have run this exercise with clients, they typically find unused reports and ones with unnecessary sections.

Suppliers and receivers (of information or whatever) benefit by jointly deciding what is needed and why. In general, flow considerations should determine how information is reported and presented.

Red Flags for Error Proofing

Over the years I have come to recognize that errors follow certain patterns. I have described them here as "red flags" to indicate that if you see these in your operations, they can often lead to an error proofing opportunity.

Symmetry. A common opportunity for error proofing occurs when multiple varieties of inputs could be made the same. Symmetry ensures the orientation is never wrong. Consider a case where there are left and right versions of a part that are otherwise identical. A common example is dress socks. Some of my dress socks have an emblem on the ankle. I generally like this feature but find it annoying when a pair of socks comes with only one emblem on each sock for the outside ankle, which necessarily designates the socks as left and right. This creates more difficulty in putting the socks on (because there are now two different socks — one dedicated to the left foot and one to the right foot). Furthermore, this causes a handling problem when laundering the socks because each pair must contain a left and a right (instead of two left socks and two right socks). By creating symmetric socks that work for both left and right feet, you eliminate the possibility of using the wrong sock or getting the wrong pair of socks if multiple pairs are mixed up.

A similar situation exists where components differ based on variations of products. For example, bed frames are typically made with bolt patterns that suit multiple sizes of beds. This eliminates the error of using the wrong input (a queen versus a single frame) and reduces inventory storage because a smaller selection of components is needed. In general, it pays to reduce the number of stock units through symmetry whenever possible.

Asymmetry. In some situations, asymmetry is absolutely necessary for the customer to get the product they want. For example, car customers expect the steering wheel of a car to be on one side or the other (depending on what country they drive in). In this situation, creating asymmetric support systems to help with identification can be most helpful. For example, a mechanic will typically refer to parts as driver-side or passenger-side, which are unambiguous. In the case of typeset letters (where you do not want letters to be put in upside down), creating an asymmetric interference so that they can only be put in with one orientation is beneficial.

My favourite example for symmetry where there should be asymmetry is credit cards. Credit cards are dimensionally symmetric but the relative location of the numbers and the magnetic strip is asymmetric. How many times have you watched a person trying to discern the proper orientation of the card when swiping? A simple solution such as a raised edge on the side opposite the magnetic strip would create enough asymmetry to help people get the swipe right. Nonetheless, we are stymied by a symmetry-asymmetry mismatch every time we have to swipe.

Direction of Flow. When looking for errors in processes, I often encounter a direction of flow problem. Consider your dishwasher. If there are a few seemingly clean dishes in the dishwasher it is not clear if they are clean dishes that need to be put away or clean-looking dirty dishes that should be part of the next load.

In heat-treat areas, parts are often annealed to relieve internal stresses in the steel. However, if the parts are annealed twice, they tend to get brittle and it is not always easy to tell whether parts have been annealed or not (see page 67). So if you see a wayward cart of parts in the area, do you risk not annealing them and have them miss an important step in the process or anneal them twice and risk making them too brittle? Having dedicated carts for unannealed parts (painted green, which is associated with un-annealed parts in heat-treat lingo) and annealed parts (painted grey) would go a long way to correcting the problem in theory. However, people often end up circumventing the colour system to avoid unnecessarily transporting empty carts. At the very least, supplying a hardness gauge to test if the parts have been annealed would be helpful, although this does not error proof the problem. The real culprit is the fact that the furnaces are situated offline and not part of the flow of the process. Attempts to create a more continuous flow will work better than creating new identifiers in this case. Offline processes with distinct input and output locations are likely the best approach to avoid the problem.

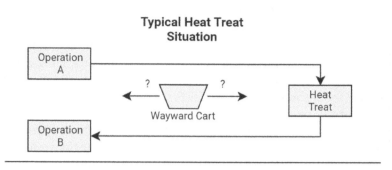

Typical Heat Treat Situation

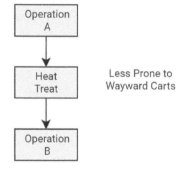

Better Heat Treat Situation

Less Prone to
Wayward Carts

Pass-through Filters. The last potentially rich area for error proofing is the realm of binary dimensional errors that can be identified by a pass-through filter. Dimensional errors refer to errors in the size and shape of a product. Process-dimensional errors occur mostly because of non-binary processes and thus do not lend themselves to error proofing per se. However, once a gross dimensional error occurs, there is typically a simple and logical way to detect it so that the error is not passed on. For example, I have seen swing-arms used to identify when full trays of parts (as opposed to the more desirable empty trays of parts) are passed to a load station. I have seen wire profiles that act like a "go/no go" gauge on the input to paint lines in the shape of the right parts isolating wrongly shaped parts. I have seen float baths and pressure tanks identify dimensional errors in different environments. The point is, if size matters, confirming the size using some physical gauge or inspection makes sense.

Limiting Variety: A Common Misunderstanding of Error Proofing

A common situation I have encountered is operations that have more than one input, and someone is tasked with deciding which one to use. For example, let's say red ribbons, blue ribbons, and green ribbons are used in batches for about an hour each (perhaps in a gift-wrapping station at Christmastime). The common practice is to have all three varieties at the station at volume so that the operator never runs out. The issue is that not only does having all three types of ribbon require more inventory at the station (and more importantly, more space for that inventory), but it creates an opportunity for the operator to take the wrong ribbon. The obvious but not common answer to this problem is to have only one ribbon at a time in the station. When I make this observation, I get a lot of responses dismissing the suggestion. These are the most common replies:

1. *We need to have all possible colours there for when the colour requirement changes so as not to disrupt the operator's flow.* All the things that disrupt the operator from their flow, such as stopping production and getting a new tote, help the operator confirm the change as opposed to wrongly continuing with the wrong colour.

2. *Bringing a new set of ribbons every time we change colour requirements increases the burden of material handling.* This is true — no contest. However, it is hard to calculate the cost in lost labour and material due to a defect of having the wrong colour (let alone the required management attention).

3. *We don't care which colour ribbon we use because we want a variety. So it is theoretically impossible to create a defect.* Saying that you want a variety indicates that too many of one colour could be read as a defect. If you want a variety then you need to specify how.

4. *The process is error proofed because we have covers on the ribbon bins indicating that the wrong colour ribbons are not to be used; thus, errors are prevented.* Covering bins not intended for use does remove the chance that they are wrongly used at the expense of more steps to open and cover bins. The operator should be focused on the ribbons, not the covers or bins.

Lean Tool: Visual Factory

In operations, not everything is equally important. Amplifying what is most important and suppressing what isn't as important often allows us to manage operations better. Visual factory is about suppressing unwanted signals (or noise) and focusing on signals that matter.

In our everyday lives, we hear a lot of noise. Whether it is traffic, the sound of birds, or the white noise of fans or air conditioners, it is difficult to suppress all of that in order to recognize audible annunciation. The situation is often worse in manufacturing environments and frenetic service environments. Not only does ambient noise cause audible signal obfuscation, but visual signals also get crowded out by distracting activity. It is best if managers eliminate as much noise and distraction as possible and create clearer signals for what is going on. The practice of colour coding (be it smocks or bins) is often misinterpreted as cutesy or decorative and thus superlative. But having every worker designation wear a specified colour helps operations if those people need to be identified quickly. For example, having maintenance wear a certain colour makes finding maintenance easier and can benefit operations because these people are often needed in urgent situations. These decisions should never be made because of aesthetics. Doctors, police officers, and fire fighters have uniforms because it makes them easier to identify when you need one of them. Dressing lunchroom staff in the same colours would be much less effective and less important to operations.

Visual factory is a term that encompasses all communication and thus tends to encompass many disparate aspects of operations as if there is no rhyme or reason to its application. The visual factory mentality should focus on what could cause the most damage the fastest, that is, eliminating unwanted noise to focusing on the visual and audible cues that are most important. When I teach lean maintenance, students normally assume that the bottleneck machines (the machines that make money) are the most important to maintain. Bottleneck equipment is in fact the *second* most important class of machine in an operations environment. The most important in every case should be machines or operations that affect safety. For visual factory, lean managers should always start with an analysis of what could cause a catastrophe if it failed. The first priority of visual factory should be to annunciate those potentially catastrophic situations and figure out how to fix or avoid them. The second priority should be the machines or operations that are bottlenecks and have a direct impact on making money. Beyond that, there is little need for visual factory and applying colour or sound differentiation would likely only cause more noise.

Managers know that some processes are more important than others and that priorities change with time. Good managers will make mental notes of inventory levels, scrap levels, and other operational data to set thresholds for when to ignore these processes and when to intervene. Occasionally, these managers will articulate such thresholds by using visual indicators (bar charts, heights of stacks of inventory or scrap as compared to wall markings, etc.) to help them quickly assess the situation. This is a fantastic practice and should be encouraged. In each case the importance of the process (for example, for safety concerns, bottleneck continuity, or flow) should be articulated as well as what the signal levels mean and how to respond to them.

These analyses are fundamental to better management of operations; when made clear, they can help more than just the individual operator or manager. By making these indicators and thresholds public, you can create a situation where even the greenest member of the team can articulate what has to happen and whether it is happening or not. This clarity often pays dividends when new employees are introduced to the process as well as when things are disrupted in operations and the process looks unfamiliar.

Finer Points of Visual Factory

Visual Cues Versus Visual Instructions

We have to recognize that visual factory is more about psychology and behaviour than the more traditional aspects of operations management and operations research. Visual factory is both a communication tool as well as a tool to solicit the right behaviour.

Operations management is often dominated by the two or three big tasks that determine flow. There are many assigned sub-tasks that seem so menial that we do not even consider them worth considering, let alone managing. Let's look at the checkout process in a grocery store. The main tasks at first glance would be calculating the amount owed, receiving proper payment and making change. However, there are additional sub-tasks, such as reaching for items to be priced, scanning them, finding codes or prices for obscure or unmarked items, placing items in the outbound receptacles (bags or the like), and handing back any change or transaction record. (A typical decision map is provided for illustrative purposes on page 72.) These menial tasks are important and help make up the process. Two checkout attendants could be equally effective at calculating the amount owed, receiving payment, and making change, but they could have much different throughput because of something as simple as deciding which items to grab first. Even being left-handed or right-handed may be a factor considering the layout of the checkout station. By focusing on the little things, we can better stabilize and improve the seemingly more important issues. However, to do this often requires a significant change in perspective before we can even recognize and analyze what is required at this seemingly insignificant level.

To improve the visual factory aspect, we want to consider where operators and customers focus their attention as this will show where we have to be more efficient. This moves from focusing on high-level concerns, but if all the steps required get done, this approach is best for efficiency and flow.

Consider the example of how most people respond to a broken door (see page 73): Leaving a building is hardly ever on anyone's list of tasks — likely because no one would expect that any thought or decision making goes into it. However, in my experience, the most common response by facilities managers to a broken door is to put a sign on the broken door that says, *Please use the other door.* And the most common response is that people see the sign and continue to use the broken door! People are not trying to spite maintenance, but it's a hardwired behavioural response to a sign on a door. The sign draws their attention and they use that very door while they try to process what they're reading. Even if there is a working door right next to the broken door, people are drawn to the sign; the

Checkout process

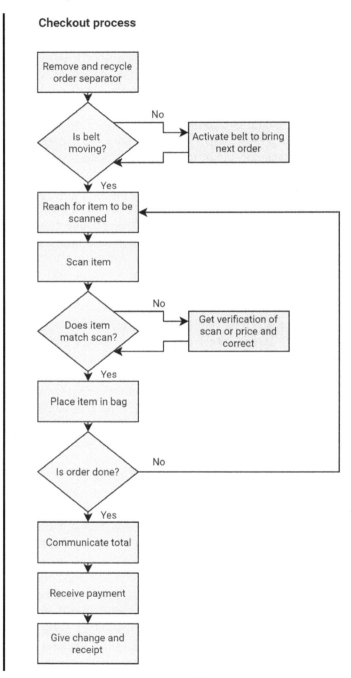

sign actually exacerbates the problem. If you were to confront the facilities managers who made the decision to post the sign, they might argue that putting up the sign was still the right thing to do (and then they will likely follow that comment with some derisory comment like "People who can't read shouldn't use doors.").

What is actually there

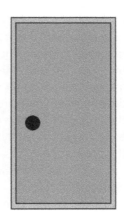

What you see

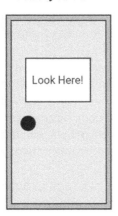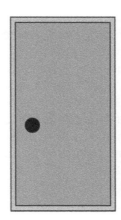

Let us analyze this in detail to see what the issues are and what else could have been done. *Please use other door* does not seem like a complicated phrase, but it is not specific as to which door one should use or why. So while it may not take much time or effort to read four words, people immediately struggle with the relevance and in response, they invariably walk into the door.

One alternative would be to simplify the message with regard to relevance by changing the sign to *Broken*. As abrupt as this seems, the message is immediately clear, and given the terseness of the language, one might be inclined to stop walking to process the message. This sign helps prevent people from running into the door but does not direct them to a usable door. What you will typically find in this situation is that the sign gets people's attention and draws them in that direction. Once the message has been processed the reader is already closer to the broken door so there will likely be disproportionately more traffic through the doors closest to the broken door. This may be OK and certainly helps curb people's propensity to walk into the door while they are processing the message.

Given people's tendency to gravitate to signs they're trying to read, another alternative is to put a sign on the door you want people to use that says *Please use this door while we repair the adjacent door*. The processing of this sign is harder but that may not matter if the sign draws the person to use the proper door while they are processing the message. As much as this would seem counterintuitive, it actually moves people where you want them faster and limits the amount of derision facility managers aim at people for doing what they naturally do.

Likely the best solution is to make the broken door look like it is broken. This can be done with caution tape, a barrier, or someone standing in front of it. These options save the need for a worded message. In the case of someone in front of the door, no one even has to know the door is broken. In all these cases, people will just recognize that there is an obstruction. Unlike signs, people naturally walk *away* from obstructions.

The point is, we often try to communicate a message through worded signs or documents when we should focus more on what is going to drive (rather than communicate) the right behaviour. We can draw on these predictable behaviours:

- People notice one-off things as long as there are few enough categories to make them exceptional.
- People walk towards worded signs (often reluctantly).
- People avoid barriers or obstructions.
- People walk away from people they do not know.
- If people are given matching connectors, they will pair and connect them (consider the tendency to attach two Lego blocks to each other).
- Matching outlines generate a mental link (when implementing kanban in an aircraft factory, we had a section of floor painted in the shape of a wing and after that no one ever asked us where they should put the wing).
- If people notice symmetry in architecture, they tend to line up along the axis of symmetry.
- "Up" is considered good and "down" is considered bad. Likewise, "green" is considered good and "red" is considered bad. (We often try to orient instrumentation dials so that the good area of the dial is painted green and points up, whereas the bad area of the dial is painted red and points down, to help people process the status.)

There are of course many more tendencies like these, but these ones come up the most in my experience. Taking advantage of these tendencies is beneficial to the effective use of visual factory and the efficiency of your operations. When considering the tasks involved for production or service delivery, we often hit a threshold beyond which there are no obvious improvements to be made to the bigger aspects of operations. However, it helps to circle back and look closely at the work environment to see both what behaviours prevail and what can be done about them. You will often be able to tie the benefit back to production or service delivery, even if you never would have seen the value if you had started there.

What Information Needs to Persist?

Another information hand-off issue that creates mismatches between message and behaviour has to do with timing. Most process designers pick up on the need to give people the information they need when they need it, but they don't always account for how long it is needed. A good illustration is how customers in a restaurant place orders (see following page). In most cases, the request is spoken and then recorded by the wait staff. At this point the wait staff has to separate out parts of the order into different packets based on who makes that part of the order — drink orders go to the bartender and food orders to the kitchen staff. Different parts of the order are needed at different times (and this is affected by how busy each area is and how many orders are already in the queue), and the order information needs to show up in different process queues. In most cases, the wait staff's handwritten note is used as a record of the order, and this paper order goes with the food so it is up to the wait staff to remember the drink order. This means that from when the customer made the order to when it is executed, information can easily be forgotten. It would be nice if the order was available in every place it was needed for as long as it was needed so nobody had to "remember" the order. And this could only work if the paper order is true to the customer's spoken order. On many occasions I have received the wrong drink item, showing the weakness of this information process. I have to wait for the bill to see if it was a mistake in initial transcription or in remembering what was written.

Another approach common in all-you-can-eat sushi places is to have the customer write down their own order (often on a check-box form that simplifies the ordering process). This has the advantage of perfect order representation (notwithstanding misunderstanding by the customer) but still may require that one of the order fillers has to read and then remember an aspect of the order.

Having the customer write down their order (thus making it more enduring than just short-term memory) is helpful, but you can take the self-service model a step further and remove the need to remember the order altogether. For example, some sushi restaurants have sushi options float by each table on little boats so that customers can see what is on offer. The customers then simply grab what they like — eliminating the need for anyone to remember the order during order fulfillment. The bill can then be prepared based on the number (and type) of empty boats at the table, which represent the orders consumed. In this case, although no measures have been taken to make the order persist longer, it doesn't matter because there is no need to remember any order; it is executed immediately.

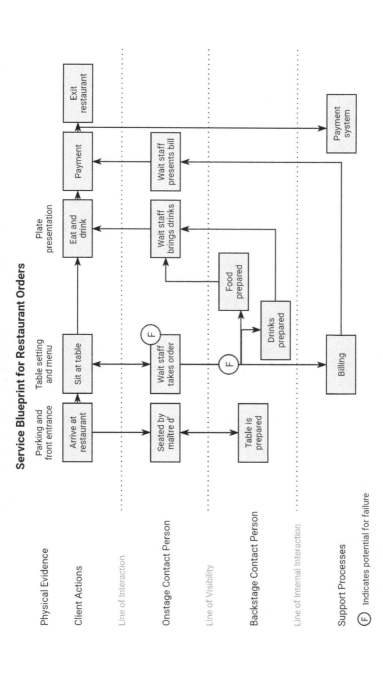

Service Blueprint for Restaurant Orders

Physical Evidence

Client Actions

Line of Interaction

Onstage Contact Person

Line of Visibility

Backstage Contact Person

Line of Internal Interaction

Support Processes

(F) Indicates potential for failure

At the end of the day, spoken orders should be eliminated if there is any requirement to remember them. After all, any order verification, confirmation, or questioning (even if not voiced) is waste. This is as true in service environments like restaurants as it is in manufacturing: Every time I ask, every time I count, every time I look up … is a waste. Where possible the process should be modified to eliminate the "remembering" requirements.

Visual Factory Simulation

One problem with visual factory that I noticed very early in my consulting is an overreliance on training to make operators conform. I noticed that management would somehow think that if only the operators would read and obey management's instructions, the visual plan would convert the workspace into a paragon of clarity and efficiency. I saw the need to wrest the domain of visual factory away from management and give it to the operators with management's consent.

A colleague of mine and I were working late one night at Seagate and we devised a simulation to illustrate the basics of visual factory. We both felt so comfortable with the simplicity of the representation that we immediately began to use it as a platform to discuss all nuances of the move to visual factory.

In the simulation, teams of operators compete against each other to complete a task using simple work instructions, and they are assessed on speed and quality of output. The output of the simulated process is a folded piece of paper with a blue line, a red circle, a diagonal green line, and a paper clip. Each team is told these are the customer requirements. The requirements are very specific about what to include but they are very vague about where these features should be and how they should be applied. We are not trying to develop any insight into process design: The simplicity of the features are not taxing on any level and closely represent the simplicity of the decisions that would normally be made in a visual factory implementation.

The other stipulation in the simulation is that only one operator can be in the operating environment at a time. Others on the team can look on and coach from a distance, but they can't be close enough to touch the operator or assist in any physical way. The team is graded on the total output of the four team members in a relay-race fashion rather than on any individual's output. The operating environment we used was consistent with Seagate's electrostatic discharge environments and clean rooms so it seemed appropriate to the participants. In fact, we also chose the environment for its isolation, which acted as a metaphor for how different shifts can affect output— something that is very common in most companies.

The other quality specification (and an important one) is that once a good part has been received by the customer, the customer assumes that all subsequent parts will be *exactly* the same. This assumption aligns with the often undiscussed expectation of operational consistency. As an illustration, consider customer perception of store shelves. Soup cans on a grocery store shelf are often displayed in multiple rows of the same soup. The customer's general expectation is that all of the cans on the shelf of the same type of soup are identical. I don't really care if tomorrow the cans are different than today (provided they still have the soup that I am looking for), so changing something on the label from yesterday to today does not bother me as long as all of the cans on the shelf on any given day look exactly the same.

This stipulation, although intuitive to customers, is often hard for the teams. At the end of the practice run, we point out the inconsistences to the team — misoriented paperclips, inconsistent placement of circles and lines, and varying marker widths — and count those issues against the team. Many find that most of the products they produced are considered failures on quality of consistency even though they meet the looser initial requirements given.

Participants sometimes squawk that if customers want a specific pattern, they should specify it. However, it does not take long to convince them that operational consistency is desirable and that they, as customers, would demand it even if not specified. Once customers accept the first product, they expect that all subsequent products must be identical.

After the practice round, teams run two rounds in full view of their competitors, during which each employee on the team takes a turn making the product. The final round scores are worth double the first round scores, and the teams are given time to adjust their environments and processes between runs. Teams generally take advantage of this time to standardize their environments so that every operator uses the same template for the circle and knows exactly where to put the paper clip (and so on) to avoid the detrimental effect of not having a consistent product. This part of the exercise alone is well worth the effort as participants are confronted with all the exogenous factors that create variability. Although we avail them of a bin full of random office supplies, most teams will restrict many items: They will often restrict the colour of paper clips and the number of markers to the bare minimum so as not to introduce variability in supply or tooling. They will use template tricks such as placing the circle template (often the masking tape roll) in the corner of the paper so that the circle's placement is consistent. To be fair, participants come up with many ideas that they could later use in improving their work environments and the solutions vary enough that you could almost do a presentation on each group's insights and responses to the simulation.

After the teams have done a practice round (with no scoring) and the first round (where they develop some improvements from the practice round and can see the score impact), we show them their first-round scores and invite them to steal ideas from other teams. However, we emphasize that if all they do is copy the ideas rather than improve on them, they cannot expect to surpass the team with the best ideas. Most teams realize how important it is to create a quality template with that first part they send to the customer. They will often have competitions within the team to decide who should be the first operator and how other operators can adjust if the first operator has to make any changes on the fly.

We then have them set up for the final round. They assume we will run the second round as we did the first. When I have done this simulation, it is often after having done other simulations where I would change the status quo in the last round in an effort to highlight a subtle but important learning point. At this point most participants are anticipating some disruption to the simulation such as me taking a marker cap away or providing a smaller sheet of paper. I don't think they usually anticipate the change we actually do make. We run the final round exactly the same as the first scored round but with only one exception: We swap the first operator with another team's. We usually have four teams competing (of maybe four members each) and we take the first operator from the first team and we switch them with the first operator of the second team, so every team is intact save an outsider as their first member. We justify this by saying their first team member called in sick or was otherwise not able to come, so a replacement was sent. We also immediately start the last round after the announcement so the teams do not have time to plan an adjustment. This small change creates havoc within teams.

As a direct result of this minor change, it becomes immediately clear which teams relied on a simplified environment to inform the operators and which relied on training. Even though the "new" member is very familiar with the product and requirements, they will not be familiar with the training that was delivered in that specific team. Thus the training investment is rendered useless (much as it would be for new recruits). Typically, the second round is won by the team whose visual factory communicated the job rather than relied on training. The learning point here is that specific task training takes time and does not guarantee success. Rather than invest in centrally designed structured training, one should invest in making the operations so simple and obvious that a monkey could do it.

In the debrief of the simulation, we focus on both what teams did to standardize their outputs and what teams did to embed the cues in the environment as opposed to relying on training. At the end of the simulation, some participants complain that we should have been transparent about the personnel switch in the final round. However, it does not take long to convince them that everyone should assume the potential of personnel change on every job. Nonetheless, managers still get caught out by this issue and use it as an excuse. Most of the learning points from this simulation reflect what has already been written: Focus on eliminating exogenous variability; consider part and information hand-off; and represent key information when it is needed in a useful form that matches the duration required.

The simulation does not introduce any universal insights (other than the need to rely on the environment instead of training) but rather awakens the discovery process for operators individually and for the group as a whole. The specifics of the simulation are flexible and can be adapted to reflect any work environment. It is well worth taking a couple of hours to run such a simulation in every situation where you want to see improvements in visual factory.

Lean Tool: 5S — A Place for Everything and Everything in Its Place

5S projects stem from the notion that an organized environment makes the work easier and improves quality. Organized environments benefit operations, but it is important to identify the purpose of the specific operations so the environment can be tailored to suit those activities.

When I worked at Seagate, 5S projects were often selected as early projects in new areas of lean because they were seen as easy. This misconception results from a misunderstanding. 5S projects are a great way to introduce neophytes to process improvement and they help create visibility and stability that can lead to success in other projects. That's the point of them. 5S projects (and all projects) are meant to either improve how the part moves through the operation or improve the capacity of the bottleneck. It is often easy (especially for 5S projects) to focus on the ancillary benefits and miss the point of the project.

5Ss stands for Seire, Seiton, Seiso, Seiketsu, and Shitsuke. The rough translation to English is Sort, Straighten, Shine, Standardize, and Sustain. However, the ultimate point of these Ss is that anything needed to get the part through the process or to keep the bottleneck working should be immediately and unambiguously available.

Some people try to use 5S to deal with disorganization or messy areas, but this manoeuvre circumvents the process-improvement aspect. For example, my desk is often messy (ask anyone); however, that's not because of a lack of a 5S project but instead the lack of a factory focus. Everything is in disarray partly because I have too many concurrent processes and can't focus my effort as narrowly.

For any 5S project, the first questions are "What products (or flows) require process improvement and where is the bottleneck?" Only then can a 5S project be defined; until that point, you are just cleaning the area and not necessarily improving the process.

Sort

The first S, — Sort — means we have to eliminate everything that doesn't benefit the operations. Of course, this includes dirt and clutter but also include things we keep in the area "just in case." The better we can agree on what the product is, the easier these "just in case" situations are to deal with. Going back to my messy desk example, if you see a stapler on my desk and ask why it's there, I might respond it's there just in case I need to staple something. It's clear that I do not know if I will need it (or even what specific task would require the stapler). If I do need the stapler, the obvious action would be to move it to where I need it most. (Where I need it most is often based on when I need it in the process of my work.) If I do not need it, it should be moved to a general area for "just in case" type stuff. The problem is that I don't know if or when I will need it, which suggests a failing in my understanding of what products I deliver.

Straighten

The second S — Straighten — refers to everything needed for a process having its place. If I know the key product processed at my desk is an expense report, my stapler is not only necessary to the process but best placed next to the printer where I will pick up the report and staple it. Through this process everything should eventually either be removed (sort) or have its place (straighten) relative to how it participates in the processing.

Red Tag Area

When starting in 5S it is beneficial to dedicate an area to the "just-in-case" type stuff. This area should be far enough away from the main process area that it becomes inconvenient to bring the items back to the process if they're not needed. The Red Tag Area is a staging area for what you are going to dispose of but you can still get it if you really need it (which overrides the inconvenience of going to get it). It is kind of like archiving a file you may or may not need. If you don't need the item for an extended period (six months is somewhat standard), you can dispose of it. If the item is required before that time, the operator or manager who is recommissioning the item needs to indicate what the item is needed for so that it can be reintroduced into the process where it is needed most.

In some cases the inconvenience of finding it and recommissioning the item is not differential enough and further inconveniences may be needed. For example, one piece of equipment was too difficult to move for the sake of Red Tagging, so rather than just unplugging the equipment I asked the electricians to remove the electrical plug. Six months later, when I told the manager in the area that we were disposing of the equipment, he claimed that his people still regularly used the equipment. When I showed him that there was no way for anyone to have powered the machine for the last six months, he was pretty convinced that the equipment could be removed without interrupting production.

The Red Tag Area is so named because part of the process is applying red tags on each of the items or equipment to indicate from where the item came, who was in charge of the area, and how it was identified in that area (i.e., name, manufacturer, and/or property identification number) as well as the date it was placed into the Red Tag Area. After the required time has expired, the area manager can be informed that the item has been out of service for said time and that the 5S team will take the next step in disposing of the equipment.

You can include other "red tag" techniques with a little bit of creativity. For example, I just read an article about cleaning your closet by first turning your clothes hangers backwards. After removing an article of clothing to wear it, you return the hanger the right way around. After a season, you'll know which items you didn't wear because their hangers are still backwards. At that point, you're pretty safe to toss them.

Shine

Once you only have the bare necessities, you should attempt to "clear" all else and "clean" the area to make all foreign objects seem out of place. That's the third S — Shine — where you get rid of anything that is not needed.

The benefit of this step is quite subtle. When I introduce Shine, I often refer to the notion that firefighters wash the fire trucks every day. I tease that perhaps that's a business opportunity for a budding entrepreneur, going around and washing all of the fire trucks for a fee. This is a canard because the purpose of washing the fire trucks is less about getting them clean and more about 1. taking the time while you are washing the trucks to inspect the trucks for leaks, scratches or abnormalities; and 2. presenting the truck in such a way that any abnormalities that develop throughout the day are immediately obvious. Shine is not about beautifying but rather making abnormality more visible.

With relatively little effort, a 5S project can create tremendous efficiency (both in the average time required to process and more notably in the variation in processing times) as well as tremendous visibility, affording others the opportunity to make process-improvement suggestions.

Standardize

Managers often find that even though everyone makes the same products, different stations (or different shifts at the same stations) will operate differently and thus will require different "straighten" rules. This leads to the fourth S — Standardize.

Standardizing the process allows for better organization of the workplace, and as more people are involved in the same process, it affords more improvement opportunities.

For example, if two operators work on different shifts and do things differently, by working together they can share knowledge of what works for each of them to develop a better standardized approach. Once implemented, you will then have two operators from which to draw ideas to further improve the now standardized process.

Standardization has to be applied operator to operator but also process step to process step. Where possible, hardware (screws, tools, fastening methods, etc.) should be standardized so that fewer tools and fewer stock-keeping units of consumables are needed.

Once an area has been standardized, it is easy to reinforce this standardization with colour cues and shadow boards. This is a good time to pull out the coloured tape to section off areas by colour and label what should go where. As well, try using peg boards for tools to promote visibility, and provide a black shadow outline to indicate when a tool is absent (shadow board), which can help motivate all participants to follow the system.

Sustain

Once the system is set up and working, some maintenance still needs to be done. Returning to the stapler example, the stapler is of little help if it runs out of staples. Rather than have staples take up space next to the stapler, we have to develop a routine so that the staples are replenished on a regular basis, keeping the stapler in a constant state of readiness. This step must be applied to all consumables and tools that degrade through wear and tear. There has to be a way to maintain this positioning for efficiency. This represents the fifth S — Sustain. Ideally, you will try to make the consumable level transparent so that anyone who sees the stapler running low on staples can replenish it, but often the job requires a dedicated periodic resource to check and replenish staples as needed.

The last part of "Sustain" considers how processes change over time. There must be an appreciation that other process-improvement opportunities exist independent of, and one must consider how future improvements will change how to sustain the situation. Part of the "Sustain" piece is an opportunity to revisit the project in light of new improvements.

Lean Tools: Checklists and Kits

In some cases, operators start sequences or tasks only to realize they are missing something and must either abort what they are doing or delay until they can retrieve what is missing. A simple pair of solutions to this problem shares elements with error proofing and with 5S: Checklists and Kitting. They are some of the easiest tools for visual factory that you can implement.

Checklists

Checklists are quite simply itemized lists of everything necessary to complete a task or sequence. When researching checklists to incorporate them into lean training at Seagate, we came across a book that carefully laid out that each item had to have a box and the box had to be ticked before the checklist was complete. I don't plan to be quite so pedantic here, but I will say that checklists have the advantage of being a temporal, unambiguous reminder of what is needed. Especially if you have gone to the effort of a setup reduction or process map, often the specifics have already been captured.

Kitting

If we take the 5S notion of "everything in its place" to its logical conclusion, we must consider the benefit of having everything in one place (and potentially mobile). Having all the tools and consumables together for a specific task can be extremely valuable and eliminates omission errors. Kits can be established on carts, in trays or even in suitcases, making them portable, which affords offline preparation. If kits are set up properly by using shadow boards and custom compartments, replenishing consumables will also be simplified, making kits a great tool for eliminating errors.

Chapter 5

The Real Process-Improvement Question

Once you feel that your company has a solid foundation in operations management and your operations are stable and transparent, you are well on your way to deciding about process improvement. However, even if you are ready, you have to be sure that others will support the initiative. You must also take into account your organization's change readiness. If, as I have suggested, you cultivated employees who gravitate to process improvement, you already have people to help you lead the change. Simpler projects like setup reduction and visual factory will help predict what parts of your organization will resist changes and in what ways. All of these insights will contribute to the success of your drive for process improvement. Had you made a decision without such insights, you would now be regretting it.

Finding Your Focus

To find your focus, the real question to answer is not what consulting company to engage or whether to do Lean Manufacturing, Six Sigma or some other regime. The real question is what part of the organization can best move the company forward. At Toyota, the front-line employee was chosen as the focus of process improvement because the front-line employee had the first impact on quality conformance and could make the most of the under-resourced operating environment. At Allied Signal (and later Motorola),

Lean Tool: Inventory Waste Reduction

There is a false debate about whether inventory is an asset or a liability. The truth is that all good inventories serve a specific purpose and the job of inventory management is to manage those purposes (as opposed to blindly managing inventory levels).

Generally inventory can be in the form of raw materials, work-in-process (WIP), finished goods (FGI), distribution inventory, or retail inventory (shelf stock). These labels simply tell us where the inventory is in the process but not necessarily a lot about its purpose to operations. To discern the purpose of all the stashes of inventory, we could start with the ideal of one-piece flow and identify all forms of inventory beyond that one-piece flow. All inventory beyond one-piece flow is a reaction to some external problem that we need to overcome — often an attempt to de-couple subsequent operations. These reactions take different, but recognizable, forms, and by understanding what we are reacting to, we may be able to find a better way to react.

Inventory Related to Setups

Batching inventory together (often for the purpose of coordinating around a setup) has two downsides: One is that the entire batch is captive while any part in the batch is being processed and the other is that the batch's flow often requires bulk handling.

- Batch inventory — One reason that one-piece flow may seem suboptimal is that our processes may dictate batches. One of the expectations of operations since World War II and likely even before that is the realization of economies of scale. It does not cost twice as much for an oven twice the size. I should be able to realize a cost advantage by employing a bigger oven to heat more than one part at a time. This scale advantage in equipment cost applies to most production equipment. However, this one-time cost advantage has to be weighed against the less-understood costs of inventory associated with the scheduling problem it creates. For example, let us say that we heat six parts in the oven at a time. If the preceding operation processes a different batch size, inventory must be stored before enough parts arrive that we can gang six of them together for the operation to work the organization focused on the design and process engineers to stabilize and improve the output through better engineering. I have been in situations where the focus went beyond the traditional choice of the operator or the engineer, but you needn't have strayed far to determine who made the difference.

Here's the thing: In order to determine the focus of your process-improvement initiative, you need to know how you make money and what stands in the way. For most manufacturing organizations, the impediment is either the bottleneck or the time to market on the next new product. Service companies are not that different: They may just emphasize information flow and better customer involvement. But in any event, analyzing the thing that constrains your company from making more money and analyzing the flows of material and information are the only ways to make an informed decision about the focus of your process improvement.

Throughput Time or Throughput Rate?

As explained in chapter 3, operations management is the study of things in business that take time where the time element matters. As long as time matters, you will want to know how long things take and what you get for that invested time. If you were to place that information on a process map, two numbers would jump out as significant: 1. How long it takes to complete the process, which is called "throughput time"; and 2. How many things can be produced in a specified time, which is called "throughput rate." Both of these numbers are significant, but you would typically focus on one more than the other depending on your desired outcome. For example, project management involves one occurrence, namely the project, and you would not likely care how many such projects could be done at one time. Your interest would be in throughput time. By contrast, if you make something in high volume, what matters is capacity, getting as many outputs as you can out of the process, so your interest would be in throughput rate. As an organization, it is important to determine whether your focus is throughput time or throughput rate so that the process improvement can best assist you. Even if you want to improve first-time-through quality (as in "efficiently." The same is true on the outbound if the following machine processes one part at a time. These inventories take up space and need to be managed. The situation described implies that all parts have the same processing recipe — the problem is made much worse if different parts have to be processed for different times or attributes. So in our oven example, if part A is in for 10 minutes and part B is in for 20 minutes, we have to wait until we get a full set of part A or a full set of part B and not necessarily the first six parts of any designation.

• Setup inventory — Whenever we perform a machine setup, the machine is effectively idle with respect to part production. To maintain continuous flow on other operations, inventory must be built up to supply the flow while the setup is taking place. As an inventory classification, setup inventory is a bit of a misnomer in that no inventory has to wait for the setup. Inventory could be processed on a different operational path rather than wait. However, for the purposes of operations management, it is beneficial to identify inventory dedicated to operations that are not operable while a setup is occurring (especially since the setup typically dictates some parameter of the inventory), and we can assume a reduction in inventory will be the reward for a reduction in setup time. In this case, we are reacting to the disruption of the setup and the need to get things up and running afterwards.

Transit Inventory

In non-trivial cases, some space is required to store inventory on both ends of a move. In some cases, this transit inventory is trapped within the operation (such as in an assembly line) where parts are at disabled stations. Reducing the transit distance and/or improving the response time of replenishment can reduce the burden of transit inventory and thus should be considered beneficial. I have been in many discussions where operations managers feel the need to put in a conveyor to bridge operations and thus "improve" processes. Conveyors create an obvious increase in transit inventory and should be avoided if reducing inventory is the goal. Moving the operations closer is the superior solution. Even if your only alternative is manual transportation, it would be better than institutionalizing a way of trapping inventory.

the case of Six Sigma), you still want to know whether to focus on throughput time, i.e., solutions that make the part quicker to make (less rework, for example) or throughput rate, i.e., a higher volume of output (better yield).

Critical path management is a tool to improve throughput time, and bottleneck management is a tool to improve throughput rate, and it makes sense to mention that the gains from process improvement will pale in comparison to the gains from simply using either of those tools. Furthermore, once you have determined whether yours is a project management problem or a capacity problem, certain process-improvement tools will stand out as being most suitable.

Process Improvement for Project Management

If your company derives its main income from projects, as is the case of building developers or research and design firms, you will likely focus primarily on how fast you can complete the project — throughput rate. Even if projects are not the main source of your money, you might occasionally look at specific projects or at departments that focus on projects, in the hopes of making the company more productive. When I worked at Seagate, a technology company, we were always focused on the project aspect of getting new products to market before competitors could. But we also knew that our bread and butter was in the volume we could sell in the window of time when we had a technological advantage (and even after competitors had caught up). So, we typically put capacity issues before project issues. However, I did use critical path management to speed up engineering approvals that had previously slowed down the introduction of new products to market. In that instance, we relied on setup reduction techniques almost exclusively. In particular, we broke down all of the tasks required to get the engineering approval complete. At each step and in order to cull superfluous activity, we assessed whether the step was value-added and necessary. We then focused on how each step could be shortened and found that the limitation was a specific set of managers with signing approval. We were able to streamline much of the approval process by revisiting the requirements for

Anticipatory Inventory

As a purchasing agent, one may often be offered discount on inputs if you place a bulk order or if the timing is particularly attractive for the seller. There is a trade-off to be considered; in some cases buying more for the sake of keeping inventory is the right decision. There are also exceptional cases when a shortage is anticipated, so buying bulk may make sense to mitigate a supply risk. In my experience, this latter scenario often applies more to maintaining inventory of obsolete equipment parts than raw materials purchases, but there are times when it just makes sense to buy more. The trade-off is the cost, space, and risk associated with holding that inventory. In each of these cases, inventory acts as an insurance policy and should be treated as such for financial purposes. The category of anticipatory inventory can be broken down further:

- Seasonal inventory — Not every business has a steady flow throughout all cycles. The most notable example is the ebb and flow of demand associated with special holidays, weather patterns, or even tax time. In fact, most industries have some seasonality — even if it means they have more demand in the middle of their day than at the beginning and end. In these cases, inventory often has to be ramped up to meet the higher demand and thus we can consider that additional demand as a function of variation in demand based on that cycle. Reducing this kind of inventory typically requires flexibility of inventory and inventory replenishment, which comes at a cost that is often easy to calculate (but a benefit that is not).
- Speculative inventory — Over and above supply advantages to buying anticipatory inventory and demand following recognized patterns, there are times when a firm wants to speculate about potential demand and maintain inventory in response. An example would be anticipating a snowstorm or expecting a surge in sales of a product when it is first introduced. In these cases, the level of inventory required will be determined partly by the aggressiveness of the manager but also by the level of uncertainty in the decision. We cannot take into account the aggressiveness of a manager, but we can attempt to address the uncertainty directly, so that the inventory level can be commensurately reduced.

approvals (in some cases allowing signatures from junior but more available managers), bundling approvals with similar key decision information to make the task of approving easier and faster for the approver, and highlighting specific urgencies for critical path approvals. I would like to say that we cut the time in half, but that was only true on average; we were still dogged by the lack of homogeneity across projects. I can say, however, that all of the project examples we addressed became faster.

Other process-improvement tools apply to project management. In some cases, visual factory techniques will be helpful. In others, a big difference comes about from examining the handling of inventory — like the inventory of approvals waiting on key desks in the above example. However, the only tool that consistently helps with project management is setup reduction (see page 99). Setup reduction will lead you to the next logical steps.

Process Improvement for Capacity

Where capacity is the intended target, process-improvement tools, such as bottleneck management, tend to affect inventory to improve capacity. This is counterintuitive because bottleneck management seems to isolate a resource as the culprit that impairs capacity without regard for the inventory around that resource. If you walk through the evolution of bottlenecks, however, you will see why we tend to focus on inventory.

If I started a company in my garage, I would likely have one of each resource — one drill, one stove, one sink, one washing machine, or whatever was required to complete the task or product. However, as I saw the potential to make more money, I would likely see the value of buying duplicate resources. For example, maybe I was constantly waiting for my product to cook or cure in an oven, so by buying a second oven I could do two batches in parallel and increase my output. Or perhaps I find that I am the limiting resource because I am running around as fast as I can and cannot do more. Getting a friend (or friends) to help would have a big impact on improving my output. These adaptations to my business would continue piecemeal until there was need for a coordinated improvement of multiple resources.

• Inventory for compensating institutional quality — Firms are often caught not meeting demand when they lose units to quality defects. When the level of quality can be anticipated, firms will often increase their supply to meet the new demand plus quality losses or demand/yield. This decision helps the firm manage the situation in the short term but creates a need for additional inventory dedicated to compensating for an anticipated loss. The problem is more insidious than your typical inventory problem because it does not just affect one location in the process or just one type of inventory but cascades backwards through the entire supply chain, creating more cost and potential instability. Managers can be forgiven for making a short-term decision to buffer inventory for yield issues but if inventory reduction is important (and when isn't it?) then quality/yield compensation has to be part of the consideration for fixing the inventory level.

Inventory for Compensating Operations Policy

Most operations textbooks do not include this category likely because it is technically covered by the other categories. However, as a practitioner it is important to distinguish areas by their potential for inventory reduction. For the previous categories, you will be able to address the size of inventory through process improvement means. This category is harder to approach if the underlying policy is not addressed. A good example of such a situation came up at Seagate. We would make many read heads (a component about the size of a flake of pepper that magnetically reads what is on a hard disk) on a single wafer much like someone would print a sheet of stamps to separate them later. Because of low yields in wafer production, we would send a sample from the wafer to the factory to see if it was worth processing the rest of the wafer. Until the sample read heads passed the test, we would withhold the rest of the inventory, which made up a significant portion. Because management wanted to save money and effort in not processing low-yielding wafers, they essentially tied up more than half the inventory waiting to see if it was worth processing. This example may seem obscure but this type of issue can manifest itself in less obvious ways, like the decision to shut down an operation during breaks when subsequent

For example, I may need a better source of electricity because I have exceeded the rating of my electrical panel and run out of room in my garage for all of my friends who are helping out. At this point, it would be time for a new location for my business. The growth process would continue until the next improvement was either too expensive or too disruptive to justify. Where I stop in this resource duplication process (or how far I have come if I am still growing) defines my current bottleneck.

You will notice in all that growth I have failed to mention how the infrastructure keeps up with the capacity improvement because (for the most part) it doesn't. As a company grows, managers and operators find ways to adapt the new resources into the process but seldom is the expansion coordinated. The net result is uneven inventory all over the plant and resources being applied to managing the inventory (expediting, storing, counting, inspecting, etc.) as opposed to making the customer happy. Even where infrastructure was redesigned to align with the new resources, other factors like machine breakdowns or worker absenteeism can reduce the benefits of intentional planning.

Any breakdown in infrastructure (waiting for a broken-down machine, conflicts in the schedule, missing operator, etc.) results in inventory which, on many occasions, creates its own disruption. In a capacity-focused situation, the amount of extra inventory is not a big deal until it creates a problem for the bottleneck. Let me clarify. If the bottleneck works at a rate of 10 good parts per minute, then the plant will produce 10 parts per minute (less any scrap post-bottleneck) as per the definition of bottleneck. If a plant has more inventory than necessary, it will take longer for the raw materials to get through the plant just as it takes cars longer on a crowded highway. However, the rate will essentially be unchanged in that you will still get the same rate of cars through the highway even if the higher volume means each car has to be on the highway for longer. On a practical level, increased inventory often creates its own problems that do affect the bottleneck rate. For example, the longer inventory sits in the company, the more chance it will deteriorate to the point where it can no longer contribute to a good part. As a result, yield may be negatively affected, reducing the number of good parts getting to the customer. Inventory also takes up physical operations are still running, which creates decoupling inventory that is solely the result of that policy decision. Focusing on other areas of inventory management may never affect this portion of inventory and thus a concerted effort to measure the effect of operational policies on inventory may be required.

Understanding the purpose of your excess inventory is the only safe way to reduce it. Unfortunately, some inventory managers see the inventory problem as an accounting issue of working capital exposure (without concern for why it is occurring) and try to cut inventory indiscriminately, which is kind of like squeezing a balloon and being surprised if the air moves to another part of the balloon (or worse yet, the balloon bursts).

The proper approach to inventory reduction is to identify the different requirements of inventory and address the main causes: for example, long setups, uneconomically large purchases, quality issues, long transits, inflexibility, and poor market information. Each one has a measurable impact on the specific category to which it is related. You may not be able to immediately calculate what a setup reduction or defect reduction plan can do to the overall inventory number but you can be quite specific about what portion of the associated category is affected.

Another approach is to reduce the inventory in an area to some low number and then actively respond to what goes wrong. The lean thinking is that inventory hides waste, so if you reduce inventory you will expose the sources of waste. The first time you do it, you will be shocked to see how easy it is to get away with less inventory. Your company will be stronger for its ability to react to what goes wrong with structural solutions, as opposed to throwing inventory at the problem. Reducing inventory through this sort of exercise can build confidence and achieve something that people thought was unachievable. (That said, doing this exercise without monitoring what goes wrong, and responding to it, is reckless.)

I have used each of these approaches with success, but I find it is important to start with an understanding of what inventory is used for. Then I recommend using a forced drop in inventory levels in situations where there is a lot of potential "just-in-case" inventory. This method will limit the things that go wrong when you reduce the inventory, as well as quickly unearth the irrational and rational reasons for why the inventory was needed in the first place.

space and can separate operators, restricting communication and feedback. Limitations in storage at convenient locations create the need for less-than-convenient inventory locations as well as extra handling, which can result in more damage and scheduling issues. In our highway analogy, it is like saying that every car runs out of gas sometime but the chances of a car running out of gas and disrupting the flow of other cars increases the longer that car has to wait on a crowded highway.

There are many examples where additional inventory creates behaviours that negatively affect the bottleneck rate and yield. This problem gets worse when different inputs complicate bottleneck schedules. Heterogeneous inputs increase work in process at the bottleneck and cause scheduling confusion or mix-ups. The solution is to get down to one-piece flow so that the waste associated with extra inventory is avoided. One-piece flow is beneficial everywhere in the company but it is especially helpful at the bottleneck that directly impacts company output.

Lean Tool: Setup Reduction

One of the most valuable and versatile tools in the entire lean toolbox is setup reduction. Setup reduction involves identifying what steps need to be done (or not) and what can be done to sharpen the focus and reduce the time required. This tool can create tremendous improvements. Setup can mean any sequence of tasks that are required in a timely manner for a desired outcome. Setup reduction can be applied to equipment that needs changeover (for example, making red pens to making blue pens), maintenance cycles (consider how a pit crew tries to minimize the time to change tires and fill the gas tank during a race), or even sequences that are required for special activities (a good example is the engineering approval process on a design change). Any sequence that requires time is a candidate for setup reduction. Cutting original setup time in half is quite common and often the target. This technique works well in manufacturing environments. It is a little more difficult to apply in service environments, but it beats the alternative service tools by a long shot. If you work in manufacturing and you are only able to do one lean initiative, I'd say 60% of the time you are best off planning for a setup reduction project; in services, I would say the applicability of setup reduction increases to 99%!

Two things must happen for the setup reduction to be an effective part of your process-improvement effort. The first is the mindset that the time the setup requires from production is the problem, not the setup itself. The second thing is a bit more subtle — the team has to *learn* from the setup reduction. Teams can realize huge benefits from setup reductions with relatively little effort, but they must avoid some pitfalls. Too often companies land on a high-capital solution, such as buying extra equipment or buying extra tooling; this way avoids addressing the real problems of the setup time loss. And too often management is put in a situation where they feel that by spending money "this one time" they can confirm their commitment to improvement and give their employees a boost. Such solutions water down the effort of the employees and torpedo any genuine effort (and potentially put management on the hook to provide the same treatment for other teams). I am happy when I hear that groups reduce an 8-hour setup to 10 minutes. I am not happy when they reduce an 8-hour setup to

0 minutes as this implies they took the easy way out and bought more capacity! That neither makes the operations more flexible (as there are always situations where a changeover is potentially required), nor does it empower the process-improvement team to do anything but spend money. Every team should be held accountable for one full setup reduction, and if there is a reason that the project they were working on gets new capacity, the team needs to find a new project.

The most obvious issue in dealing with setup reduction is the idea that the setup is the problem and eliminating waste from the setup will not have any real effect. For example, if a stamping machine uses a different die for left-side and right-side components, the required changeover from one die to another will seem like the problem. Schedulers will indicate that the time required (let's say 8 hours) is too long. They will want to change the schedule to include longer runs, thus amortizing the setup time over more parts, which requires carrying more inventory; they will argue this justification to get around the problem. Of course, this is not the only way to address the problem. An alternative solution would be for the schedulers (or other operations people) to work with maintenance technicians or other tradespeople they do not normally work with to try to reduce the amount of time the changeover takes. To schedulers, this interaction might seem a lot harder because it is outside their regular operations. But when we start identifying the specific activities that go on during setup, we almost always find that there is a lot of waste in the process and thus we can reduce this time. The mindset has to change from the setup or changeover being the problem, to which we respond with a bad scheduling solution, to the waste in the setup being the problem. Eliminating waste allows us to be more flexible in scheduling and reduce inventory.

There are five basic steps to a setup reduction project:
1. Capture the steps that have to happen or what is happening.
2. Compartmentalize steps and assign them to tasks that have to happen.
3. Categorize each task as an internal or external activity.
4. Coordinate smaller projects to eliminate the unnecessary tasks and shrink the others.
5. Test run and go back to step 1.

The last step implies that the project is never done, but this assumption is only partially true. In my experience, setup reduction projects are initiated through acute need or desperation and are often shepherded by someone quite senior and influential. As improvements are made, this leader will often shift attention to other key areas and leave the follow-on improvements to a lower level process owner. For the leader of the project you could say the project was a success even though the project is never really complete from the standpoint of the process owner. This is consistent with the plan-do-check-act cycle commonly associated with lean.

When teaching setup reduction, I intend to help each group with their own setup situation. However, for the purposes of teaching the basics, I typically take the class out to the parking lot and have a volunteer change the tire on my car. The premise is that I would like to minimize the time I lose while the car is idle. This includes all the time the car is unsafe to drive (no tire, car jacked up, etc.) as well as the time required to make the car drivable again. Clearly, no project was focused on changing a tire but rather shortening a setup, speeding through a preventive maintenance procedure, shortening the time required for approvals, or whatever. However, the tire change as a setup example and the car as the metaphor for a machine seem to work well. I will use this setup as an example to illustrate all of the steps and subtleties of setup reduction.

Step 1: Capture

This step has become immeasurably easier with video technology. Once "capture" meant following operators or technicians around and writing down everything they did (in real time!). Thankfully video can now be used to capture tasks and is often aided by a built-in timer for accurate recording of sequence and duration of tasks.

This step's purpose is to list all of the events that actually happen. Quite often I hear managers and operators say, "I can tell you what happens; why do you need to capture it on video?" The reason is that in more than 20 years of doing setup reduction, I have yet to watch a video playback where someone didn't say, "I didn't know I (or we) did that!" So take the time and the political flak and make sure you capture the process on video! Back in the days of VHS tape, I asked the operators to store the tape for me so they knew I was not using it for anything other than improving the process. (This was often a concern, particularly in union environments.) It's important to keep in mind that the lean practitioner is only a facilitator. The insights come from the operators seeing themselves doing things (right or wrong) and how much time each step takes. In other words, there is no need to look at the video except when watching it with the operator. In the days of digital video, it can be hard to convince operators that you do not have a second copy, but it is worth your while to convince them that the process is driven by their input (not yours). If I know I can transfer the output to a larger format for proper viewing, I often suggest that I create the video on the operator's own phone to allay any fears that I will be using the video for any other purpose.

In the tire change simulation, we start the clock when the car is stopped and the driver turns the car off. The clock does not stop until the driver is back in the driver's seat and turns the car back on after the new tire is safely installed. Deciding the specific starting and ending points for your setup is very important and often creates a debate along the lines of labour demarcation. In manufacturing, what we are really trying to capture is the time between when the last good piece is produced from one production run to when the first good piece is produced from the next production run after the setup. This of course implies that if qualification has to be done before the parts are considered "good," it too must be considered part of the setup. This makes some people uncomfortable because it is dependent on things out of their control, but the only way to gain control of the entire setup is to include it. Alternatively, there could be some steps that make the qualification longer and negate the advantages of other improvements. In the end, everyone must be comfortable that a reduction in the setup time has been defined, given that the project should benefit everyone.

In the simulation, the video follows the driver as they exit the car, remove the tire and hardware from the trunk of the car, jack up the car, remove the old tire, mount the new tire to the hub, return the tire and hardware to the trunk, and restart the car. Typically this takes just under 20 minutes. I have listed these steps because they are what you would expect to happen. If that was all that happened, one might be forgiven for not capturing the event on video. There are a few other things that happen just about every time:

1. Drivers rush to get the tire and hardware out of the trunk only to find themselves sitting on the ground reading the instructions on how to change a tire.

2. Drivers will position the jack on the ground, uncertain if it is in the correct or safe position, and they will lose time assessing the situation they have created. (This situation is made worse by the fact that they know they are being filmed.)

3. Drivers will raise the car using the jack to the point where the tire spins freely and then realize that it is easier to loosen the tire lugs when the tire is still touching the ground and cannot spin.

4. Knowing they are being timed, the drivers will hurry when turning the screw jack, almost to the point of exhaustion, but they waste time trying to find where they left the lug nuts, a search that can take more time than it took to raise the car.

5. As they replace the tire and hardware in the trunk, they either quickly throw things in, leaving a mess for anyone who has to use the tools later, or they put the tools away neatly only to find they missed one and have to start over.

I mention these points not to embarrass or belittle the volunteer drivers but to make the point that there are many things that get captured on video that can help with the analysis — the video does not lie. None of these foibles would be considered if the sequence was dictated. Each offers an opportunity for significant reduction in setup time.

Step 2: Compartmentalize Steps and Assign Them to Required Tasks

After watching the tire change, one usually has a jumbled notion of the tasks to be accomplished. Luckily, the simple exercise of writing these tasks down will help us organize them so that we can make sense of what has to happen. While the tire change is going on, I have students with clipboards keep track of what tasks have to happen and how long they take. This is the way industrial engineering was done before video capture, but the students quickly realize how futile that exercise is and how much they will have to rely on the video capture to correct their notes. Nonetheless, the clipboards usually are a good starting point. For example, one might list these tasks:

20 seconds: get out of car

1 minute: empty trunk

2 minutes: place jack and raise car

4 minutes: check and adjust jack to the right position

30 seconds: turn lugs

1 minute: lower car

2 minutes: remove lugs

Etc.

Some basic groups of tasks should form the structure. For example, the driver needs the equipment (spare tire, jack, lug wrench, etc.) available before work can begin. So "empty the trunk" seems reasonable because the order of the individual activities within that task is less important than when the step itself is done. Including activities related to jacking up the car in this first task would be a mistake because jacking up the car requires the jack to be available; they should be part of different tasks. Whether the walk from the driver's seat to the trunk is included in emptying the trunk or not does not seem important, but it is good to keep it as a separate task because it has to be done first (at least in the current process).

Many people ask about parallel operations. If the operations are done by more than one person in parallel, they should be represented as such, but often the setups are only done by one technician, so they should be recorded the way they are done and not represented in the way they "should" be done.

When complete, this activity should result in a list of tasks in order, along with the actual time taken for each step. Observers may argue that there were one-off situations that are not representative. For example, when the driver takes time to read the instructions many recorders argue that the driver would not have to do that when required to change a tire in the future. You can always dismiss a timed task once it is recorded if the dismissal is justified but not recording it makes a potential problem invisible.

Video capture of people can create its own problems. When consulting, I once captured a manual slicing process in a food service company. The operator saw the camera and asked if she could have some time to put on make-up. I said that I had no issue with that but the video was not meant to capture her (at least not her face), only the process steps. When she started, she indicated that one of the steps had taken longer than normal and asked if she could start the video over. I indicated that I only needed to get a good capture of the full process — not necessarily the fastest run of a good process. I continued by saying that I would look at the times, but typically only a few of the timed sequences really matter. Whether she had done her fastest or slowest would not matter unless that sequence was one of the key ones. Even in those cases we could have a competition to see who was the fastest at those and record those times to see if it changed the setup time significantly. As I had indicated previously, some of the earliest resistance will come from the person being filmed because of their concern that they are letting the company down due to a foible. The stress should be placed on capturing the regular process (not the process as performed by an obvious neophyte or a world champion!).

At this point in the tire change simulation, you should have a video with a time signature and that should be used to create a set of steps and times somewhat like the one on the following page.

You will notice that some tasks repeat themselves. Tasks like "put stuff back in trunk" had to be interrupted and restarted because it only became clear that the jack must be lowered further (much lower than is required when removing it from under the car) to fit it into its designated place while in the process of putting everything back in the trunk.

Getting this first good capture of steps is important. You can always discuss the relevance of some of the steps you have included and even remove steps that are incidental but it is important to get one comprehensive list before you take such action.

Time	Elapsed Time	Step
0:03	0:33	Walk to trunk
0:36	1:01	Empty trunk
1:37	0:25	Place jack
2:02	3:55	Read instructions
5:57	1:22	Place jack
7:19	2:41	Raise car
10:00	0:12	Turn lugs
10:12	0:19	Lower car
10:31	1:53	Loosen all lugs
12:24	0:28	Raise car
12:52	0:14	Remove tire
13:06	0:08	Bring good tire from rear
13:14	0:28	Lift tire onto hub and align
13:42	0:03	Place top lug to secure tire
13:45	0:31	Place all lugs and finger tighten
14:16	0:45	Use wrench to tighten lugs
15:01	0:18	Lower car
15:19	0:35	Use wrench to tighten lugs
15:54	0:22	Lower jack
16:16	0:52	Put stuff back in trunk
17:08	1:17	Lower jack
18:25	0:12	Put jack and everything back in trunk
18:37	0:22	Walk to driver's seat
18:59	18:56 Total	Start car

Step 3: Categorize Each Task as an Internal or External Activity

Some of the tasks cited have to be done while the equipment or operations are "off" (in our case, when the car is off) and some can be done while the equipment or operations are active and running (even though we have chosen to do them while the car is off). We call steps that are done while the equipment or operations are off as internal to the setup. Those steps that are not internal are external to the setup.

By using this separation, we can scrutinize each task to see if all of the internal steps need to be internal. For the tire change example, the car is not active while the tire change hardware is being removed from the trunk: That step is internal. However, if we relocated the equipment so that it was "out of the trunk," we would not have to take time while the car is off to remove items from the trunk or place them back. Realistically, just by relocating the equipment to outside of the trunk we could gain back the 1:01 step of walking to the trunk and at least some of the 0:52 + 0:12 time of putting things back in the trunk from our setup.

Once we look at accommodating these changes we often realize that some internal tasks can be made external. Furthermore, as we start these discussions not only is it clear that some tasks can be made external but that some tasks have needed revision for years and only now that we look at them in the context of what has to be done do we realize they can be streamlined or even eliminated with very little effort.

Step 4: Coordinate Smaller Tasks to Eliminate the Unnecessary Steps and Shrink the Others

After we sort the tasks, we will see that there is a lot of time when we were forced to stop operations to accomplish certain ancillary tasks. By eliminating these tasks or stopping operations less frequently, we can cut the time required. (See the revised list of tasks on page 108.)

Time	Elapsed Time	Step	Internal	External
0:03	0:33	Walk to trunk		0:33
0:36	1:01	Empty trunk		1:01
1:37	0:25	Place jack		0:25
2:02	3:55	Read instructions		3:55
5:57	1:22	Place jack		1:22
7:19	2:41	Raise car	2:41	
10:00	0:12	Turn lugs	0:12	
10:12	0:19	Lower car	0:19	
10:31	1:53	Loosen all lugs	1:53	
12:24	0:28	Raise car	0:28	
12:52	0:14	Remove tire	0:14	
13:06	0:08	Bring good tire from rear		0:08
13:14	0:28	Lift tire onto hub and align	0:28	
13:42	0:03	Place top lug to secure tire	0:03	
13:45	0:31	Place all lugs and finger tighten	0:31	
14:16	0:45	Use wrench to tighten lugs	0:45	
15:01	0:18	Lower car	0:18	
15:19	0:35	Use wrench to tighten lugs	0:35	
15:54	0:22	Lower jack	0:22	
16:16	0:52	Put stuff back in trunk		0:52
17:08	1:17	Lower jack		1:17
18:25	0:12	Put jack and everything back in trunk		0:12
18:37	0:22	Walk to driver's seat		0:22
18:59		Start car		
	18:56	Total	8:49	10:07

The simple act of moving the storage location of the "stuff in the trunk" and having it ready ahead of time cuts our operation's downtime in half. (In our example, there are around 9 minutes of internal activities that we should keep internal and 10 minutes of internal activities that we could move to external after relocating the "stuff in the trunk.") Note: We will never be 100% accurate with the times, and we cannot be sure to have a 10-minute improvement, but even if one or two activities were a little bit faster or slower than we predict, the overall benefit of a faster setup would still be realized.

It is not trivial to make this change, but the change itself is quite reasonable. In some scenarios, the benefit is not realized by changing the storage locations, like in the tire change example, but rather through coordination (making sure the crew making a change is ready with the tools before the operator shuts down the operation) or increasing spares (having a good part ready to replace a part that has to be cleaned or adjusted so the cleaning or adjustment can be done offline). A lot of the benefit is anticipating when you need stuff and having it ready. The projects required to make internal activities external are usually quite simple and do not typically affect other operations. Nonetheless, a discussion and some deliberation are warranted.

There are often also opportunities to do internal activities in parallel, which often means employing more manpower, but this can be justified by a reduction in internal time. For example, aligning the tire to the hub orientation cannot be done until the car is raised. But one worker can lift the tire to the approximate height and orientation (line up the top hole to the top lug) while another worker removes the old tire so that once it's off, the new tire can be put on more quickly.

The last opportunity to reduce setup time comes from shrinking the time of the internal activities. The most effective way to do this is to target manual adjustment. For example, when you watch the video of the worker/driver jacking up the car, they typically turn the jack screw quite quickly for a while and then stop to see if the car is high enough. They will often do this in three or more bursts of energy, losing time each cycle when they stop and check the height. They also sometimes lose track and jack the car too high, requiring more internal time to lower the car later. Rather than have them continue raise-check cycles and lose time each cycle, they should count how many turns it takes to raise the car to the optimal height and then only do that many turns (no adjustments). Furthermore, when we count these turns we find that the number is unnecessarily high because the jack's starting height is so much lower than the car's initial position. We can reduce the number of turns of the jack screw if we place the jack on some platform (a phone book has often been effectively applied in this regard) so that we can have the same effect with fewer turns and not compromise safety. Likewise, we also know how many turns are required to lower the car (same number as it took to raise it) and we do not have to employ a check and adjustment cycle on the way down either.

Coordinating part hand-off and setting orientation are also good ways to shave time. I have witnessed many examples where the part is handed to the operator upside down or in some orientation that must be adjusted before it can be used. This mistake at best creates another step for the operator and at worst creates confusion. For example, in the tire change exercise, the fastest teams have invariably thought about how to orient the tire so that it has the best chance to smoothly go on the lugs. The alternative is to take the heavy tire and randomly press it against the lugs — twisting and adjusting the tire left and right until the lugs line up. This "adjustment" sequence lasts around 20 seconds. Twenty seconds does not mean much to a 20-minute tire change but if you are trying to get under 2 minutes, 20 seconds is a big waste.

Some teams consider making sure the car is stopped in a position where one lug is top dead centre so that they can predict (rather than look for) the lug orientation. This idea makes a lot of sense but the practicality of stopping a car in a specific tire orientation may cause its own problems and becomes situation specific.

Another way around the lug issue is to create a new symmetry where the tire orientation does not matter. In car racing they often migrate to a single lug/hub system where the tire orientation does not matter. Creating symmetry to eliminate orientation steps is something I always consider in lean projects.

Projects like this one can benefit from tools, fixtures, or instructions that eliminate guessing or adjustment. The net effect is a setup change where the internal time is significantly less than originally conceived. At this point, it is important to test run the improved setup regime to see if any new issues were introduced and to see if all workers benefit from the new set of tasks. (Testing it with new workers often creates more ideas for other projects that could reduce the internal time further.)

Step 5: Stabilize the New Setup Process

Once all workers have had an opportunity to improve the setup, it is important to change the current documentation to reflect the changed procedure. This update helps ensure that new operators are trained on the new setup and changes in other processes recognize these changes.

There is an opportunity to use power tools to improve the setup further but it is important to go through the five steps without introducing new power tools as their introduction tends to hide opportunities to make the setup better. The analysis should always be consistent in that it is applied to the current set of operators and the current level of tools. Once step 5 has been reached it may be worthwhile to introduce mechanically faster ways of doing the tasks we eventually decide to keep and maybe even segment the workforce to have only the fastest of workers do specific setups. All of this should be predicated on the resulting process and how important continuing to save time is compared to other opportunities for the same resources. A setup that was devastatingly important when it was 10 hours may not be worth improving after the setup is reduced to 20 minutes! There are some setups that you will want to drive down to zero but there is limited return every round of improvement. You will likely want to apply your effort where you will get better returns rather than work towards a zero setup in every case.

In fact, one of the best benefits from setup reduction is not the time saved but the opportunity to do the setup more often! This sounds completely counterintuitive but once your setups are low, you will have a new outlook on how to run your business. For example, no one relishes changing their car tire because they know it will take about 20 minutes. However, if you could get that to under 2 minutes (very common in my experience with the tire change simulation), there may be benefits to doing a tire change regularly so you do not get a flat tire. Changing the frequency can create stability (especially when the time between products is so small that you can run batches of one) and actually improves the ability to do the setup because it is more familiar. Maybe the reason we take so long to do a tire change is because we only do it every five to ten years!

Operations Transparency Through Inventory Reduction

Lean manufacturing not only sees inventory as trapped and perishable working capital but as a screen hiding improvement opportunities. High inventory levels hide operational issues. This is true of production (for manufacturing) as well as order fulfillment for services. When we think of built-up work-in-progress (WIP for short) inventory, we assume we are talking about an inanimate input to the process that takes up space. The space that it takes creates a barrier to better layouts and communication among workers. We don't normally think of customers as inventory, but if there is a queue of customers waiting on orders, we have to consider them inputs to the system and we have to recognize that they are perishable — the wait could negatively affect their orders and/or cause them to leave. But having customers waiting can affect other operations with a whole new set of problems. Customers who feel they've waited too long in line are harder to serve effectively than a customer who did not have to wait. As well, parts do not get upset if some have been expedited, but if you serve later customers before finishing with earlier customers, you might create some ill will. And, finally, long lines put pressure on servers to cut corners or dismiss defects while trying to serve the customer quickly. Even though the aspects of the "'inventory" in each case are quite different, the principle of inventory causing waste and creating problems still applies. For this reason, reducing inventory (and long queues of customers) is important for operational stability.

Before making the all-important decision about how to formalize your commitment to process improvement, you should have low enough inventory (of all sorts) and stable enough operations that you can sense what your main problems will be. Setup reduction, visual factory (including 5S), and error proofing help in this goal of reducing inventory for more operational stability and can be done regardless of what process-improvement regime you decide to use. In fact, using them will help you decide what process-improvement regime you should use. So, at this point you should have these standards set:

1. Your operations should be stabilized sufficiently that you can discern the strengths, weaknesses, and key needs of your operations (typically including the identification of the bottleneck and/or longest lead process).

2. Management should appreciation what improvement efforts are already afoot and the capabilities of the employees leading them.

3. The team should understand whether the most improvement can come from operator input, better design for manufacturing, better execution of moving customer-focused designs to fulfillment, or more control from middle management.

Lean Tool: Visual & Physical Signalling, or Kanban

One of the best ways to minimize waste in an operation is by using one-piece flow, which is essentially the thought behind kanban. Kanban is the brainchild of Toyota's Taiichi Ohno, and it originated during a tour he took of North America to get ideas on how to improve his car factory. Ironically, the idea of kanban did not come to him when touring a competitor's factory but rather when he was buying bananas at a Piggly Wiggly grocery store. As the story goes, Taiichi Ohno noticed that the store would only display a limited number of bananas and stored the rest. Once a bunch of bananas was purchased, the hole in the display would signal an attendant to add more bananas from storage.

Kanban loosely translated from Japanese means signal-card and the concept is that the production schedule should not be fixed in time but rather a result of a dynamic pull signal, like the void in the banana display. Some of the most successful and easy-to-manage kanban systems are quite literally a parking spot for the part. The parking spot is used to signal when to produce the next one. If the part is in the parking spot, the operator is instructed to stop and only start producing that part when the parking spot is empty.

Parking spots, although very effective, are not a perfect match for every inventory situation. For example, if parts are made in batches, supplying one part means supplying many parts at once and this requires a lot of parking spots! To get around these issues, there are other kanban systems that use cards to represent inventory demand. In these scenarios, a part is only authorized to move when it is accompanied by a card. Once the part is used, the card makes its way back to where the part was produced, so it in effect represents an order for a new part. The card accommodates more mobility than a single parking spot (including the ability to change destination stations), and the number of cards can be increased or decreased to manage inventory on a macro level. As well, the card can be marked with part information, locations, instructions, and priority — all of which are not as possible with parking spots. However, given that the card represents control over scheduling, people tend to hoard cards to manipulate the schedule as they see fit. For example, a supervisor who knows that part XYZ is always in demand at the end of the week will store the card in his office until someone screams for the part and then he'll send the card back into the system and look like a hero. This undoes the benefits of a kanban system.

Of course, the "cards" do not need to be cards or even card shaped, although cards are one of the cheapest and easiest things to produce in a pinch. The signals (or cards) can be almost anything marked to represent the part it is scheduling. Examples abound of ping pong balls being used for kanban signals (with ping pong ball transfer systems such as tubes to return the balls). Totes or containers can be used as well as they naturally move with the part and often recycle to the production area. Using a tote or a bin is a lot like a parking spot but the parking spot has the ability to move and contain the product.

As demand increases or as the number of operations to be fed increases, the kanban system can be tweaked to accommodate the situation with the introduction of new cards. This tweak, of course, comes at the expense of system complexity. However, the advantage of having a dynamic schedule that responds to real usage far exceeds the static schedule alternatives.

Raceway Kanban

One of the disadvantages of kanban is that it does not deal with stock-keeping units proliferation all that well. In some cases the number of stock-keeping units in the system makes the kanban system more difficult to design and maintain. For example, if I have four different stock-keeping units feeding my operation, I will likely need a kanban system for each, thus quadrupling my potential inventory at each stage. One way to get around this issue is called a raceway kanban. In a raceway kanban, successive operations are grouped so that one kanban is needed at the beginning and one at the end, which alleviates the need for the necessary variety of inventory in the raceway. Consider a company that makes four colours of markers. Once the colours have been defined, five successive operations affect each of the colours. Let's say we have established a safe inventory for each of the five operations is 12 markers. We would need 12 each of the red, 12 blue, 12 yellow, and 12 black markers on standby and at the first operation following the point where the colours are defined. So if I use a blue marker in that first operation, a signal would go back to produce a new blue marker to replace it. Similarly, a red, yellow, or black marker would be produced to replace any that were pulled to the next operation. The next operation would also have 12 of each colour and operate under the same rules so that any marker pulled to the next operation would signal a pull from the previous operation of the same colour. None of these operations treats the markers any differently; they could involve the application of a generic label but it would still involve some processing. In this case, we would have 12 markers as inventory for each colour for each of five stations, making a total of $(12x4)x5=240$ markers. By having a kanban for each colour at the end (signalling the raceway of five operations) and one at the beginning (feeding the raceway), you can cover all possibilities. Between the operations (within the raceway) you will only need a colour-blind single kanban if at all as the operations in the raceway work on the next piece regardless of colour, so they need no additional inventory. The final operation has 12 of each colour to support the customer and if any get pulled, a signal would go back to the operation where the colour is defined and that colour marker would be replaced. That marker would go through all five operations successively without stopping in any kanban until the end. Given the longer processing time, the final kanban may be made larger but even if it doubled to 24 per colour there would still be a reduction of inventory from 240 markers to $(12x4)x2$ or 96. You can see that as the number of SKUs increase, this technique becomes more effective at reducing inventory.

The Problem with Buffers

Many process-improvement practitioners use kanban extensively as it is a great tool for reducing inventory. I am much more impressed with kanban's ability to create smoother flow. (Smoother flow always has the effect of naturally reducing inventory.) It is for this reason that I find the tool so valuable around the bottleneck.

Too often when I discuss kanban, people who know it start to ask me how to calculate the buffer sizes. There is a formula for calculating optimum buffer size based on lead time, costs, and operational confidence, but I find it counterintuitive to come up with a static number to optimize not only a dynamic system but one that we are using to improve the process over the long term. This discussion has gotten me in a fair bit of trouble over the years. One time I was called in by a window manufacturer to teach them all the ins and outs of kanban and they pretty much drummed me out of town because they were only looking for a better formula (which I dared to tell them did not exist). All of my suggestions that their problems stemmed from a misapplication of kanban were seen as me not knowing how to do math or use the formula properly.

The formula they were referring to is called the formula for economic order quantity (with a safety buffer). The premise is that order costs are affected by the quantity ordered and by optimizing the order quantity you can minimize the order costs. To be specific: Every time I make an order there are costs in processing the order. The costs can include surcharges, labour time and effort on my part, shipping costs, receiving costs, banking fees, and accounting. Theoretically, these costs are the same per order regardless of the quantity. If these order costs, S, represent all order costs per order (a fixed cost), we can recognize that our annual order costs will increase with the frequency of orders. In fact, if we can approximate the annual demand, D, for the part we are ordering (another fixed number), we can consider an order quantity of Q and approximate our annual order costs at the number of orders we make per year (D/Q) multiplied by our fixed order cost, S. Clearly we can reduce our annual order costs by making each order larger (in this case, a bigger Q) to the point where we order the entire annual demand all at once and only have to pay the order costs once per year.

This makes sense until we realize that there are costs for holding inventory. Given that some inventory is perishable (goes bad, becomes obsolete, or gets damaged), requires storage (in some situations, an air-conditioned space), and costs money (incurring some finance costs among other costs), we actually want to order less each time to not incur higher holding costs. If we can assume that there is an average holding cost per part that we can apply to this decision, we can compare the holding costs to the order costs to minimize our costs relative to order sizes. It would make more sense to consider a part storage cost per day as the inventory amounts change daily, but this would be arguably quite small. Nonetheless, we could multiply this daily cost to get an annual cost by which we could multiply the annual inventory average to get the annual storage costs (or as they are referred to more commonly, holding costs). So let us say h is the cost of holding a single unit of inventory for a year (storage, handling, and financing included).

Calculating the average inventory costs relative to the order decision is quite easy. We will always have some "safety" inventory around so that we never run out, but above that we will receive our order quantity and will expect to receive the next order quantity just as the level of inventory goes back to that safety level. The net difference between the safety level and peak is the order quantity. The difference between the beginning of the period and the end of the period is Q, and if we can assume that the rate of depletion is somewhat regular, the average amount at any given time is the average of Q (at the beginning of the period) and zero (at the end of the period), or just $Q/2$. Thus our annual holding cost for any part we are ordering is $h \times Q/2$.

To optimize the order size, we want to minimize the annual order costs (i.e., $S \times D/Q$) and the annual holding costs (i.e., $h \times Q/2$). At this point, we can try a few values for Q to see which costs are higher or lower or we can go into Excel and use the solver function to optimize these two. I think this manipulation is healthy as it gets us thinking about where the costs are and what the differences are. I always recommend that people look at what the costs are and what kinds of cost differences are generated at different order volumes.

However, anyone who studied first-year differential calculus can see that there is a function with which we can calculate the optimum value. As much as this sounds good (read: easier), it actually takes managers away from better understanding the numbers.

I will dispense with the differential calculus derivation to present the final formula:

$$EOQ= \sqrt{\frac{2DS}{h}}$$

So, simply put, we can take two times our annual demand of product times the cost per order, divide by the annual holding cost per part, and then take the square root of the whole thing to get our economic order quantity.

When I teach operations management and I get to this point, the students usually breathe a sigh of relief as if they now have the answer. I then take them through a simple example to show them how ridiculous that answer could be. I work with the idea of using an ATM as everyone is familiar with that process. I ask them to list the costs in holding the money; immediately, they say that I do not receive interest on money in my pocket, so the cost of carrying money must be the foregone interest the bank offers on my savings account. Thankfully, h is unit cost per year, so plugging in that figure is simple. When I ask them about order costs, they tend to think that there aren't any because ATMs are so common. I then point out that if I am teaching (which at the time I actually am) and I wanted money, there are no ATMs in the classroom. So I begin a mock auction to see how much I would have to pay someone to go to the bank machine and retrieve my money. Usually, the price settles around $0.50, which I argue would be a realistic order cost to cover the cost of going out of your way to find an ATM, and there is even an argument that it could be higher because some banks or ATMs charge $0.75 or more if you are not using your own bank's ATM. I suggest that I take out a total of $10,000 per year from the ATM, so that is a nice round number for my annual demand or D. Interest rates have gone up and down over the years but even if we consider a low holding cost of 1%, the failings of the formula will be clear. I have them run the numbers with D=$10,000, S=$0.50, and h=1%. I get the unanimous answer of $1000. When I ask them how many take out $1000 every time they go to the ATM, none respond ... And then I see them experiencing that Ah-ha! moment.

When I ask them how much they feel is the right amount to take out of an ATM, most say $200 or less. They argue that we were just making estimates so we can expect the number to be a little off, but I counter that to get the EOQ down to $200 we either have to raise the holding costs to 25% or have them make the order costs only $0.02! They typically say that they do not take out $1000 because they will spend it right away, with which I agree: The holding cost is higher than the 1% interest (because of the potential for theft and loss while it is in your pocket) and variable in that the more cash they have, the faster they will spend it.

I then go back and point out that we thought our estimates were very reasonable, and estimates we might make for obscure products in a manufacturing setting with which we are not familiar would not be any more accurate. In fact, we are likely to make more estimation errors in the product calculations and be much less likely to notice that the EOQ calculated is just ridiculous in that situation. The EOQ formula removes us from the numbers so we really do not understand what the EOQ output actually means.

What is worse is that even if the number is accurate, it institutionalizes the order quantity so that we have less incentive to reduce order costs (such as when our order costs are a long setup on a machine) or holding costs (losing the benefit of, for example, ordering so little that we can keep all of the inventory at the station that uses it). In fact, using the EOQ value can actually discourage us from further process improvement! If the purpose of kanban is process improvement, using the EOQ formula religiously is the worst thing you can do.

I have omitted a lot of discussion on kanban and EOQ but I do this on purpose. I feel readers are best served by focusing on flow and monitoring the raw numbers for opportunities rather than institutionalizing buffer values and desensitizing the inventory impact with a fancy formula. Inasmuch as kanban can help you create flow and lay bare the inventory values, it can be a great tool.

Chapter 6

The Strategic Component of Process Improvement

Where Centralized Leadership Fits

Before management commits to a process-improvement initiative, there has usually been prior discussion about the desired outcome. If not, consistency and continuity demand some discussion of what the future at the firm will look like if the initiative is successful.

The academic literature on strategy discusses whether exploring new strategies or exploiting current strategies is a better use of time, and the answer is "it depends." Consider an analogy about looking for the highest mountain peaks. You can exploit your surroundings to continually ascend until you are at the highest relative point. Alternatively, you can leave your current position and fly around exploring potentially higher starting positions. Starting from the new location could lead to a higher point than was possible locally. Discussions about exploring tend to cause more dissent because there is so little information to use and so many ways to interpret information. Everyone can objectively assess what relative improvement means but interpreting far-off clues is more subjective.

In relation to process improvement, the exercise of exploring is best led by one person so as not to muddle the effort. Business history is rife with examples of individuals who have led their companies to new lucrative strategies while suppressing the input of others — think of Steve Jobs from Apple or Sam Walton of Walmart. Most certainly, when adopting a process-improvement initiative, a company has exhausted most of its exploiting opportunities and needs to explore new strategies. It is up to management to establish parameters for the exploring exercise and metrics on which to measure the exploring outcome. Once that has been done, it is best to designate a visionary leader to guide the company to the new world of process improvement without further interference from management.

Designating a leader sounds counterintuitive: Isn't process improvement the culmination of many people working on many projects to better the company? It is, but for the sake of clarity and consistency, direction and messages should come from a single source.

Two things must occur immediately at the start of a process-improvement initiative or the initiative will be compromised:

- All stakeholders must envision a future where they see their role and on what basis they can contribute; and

- The vision must be consistent for all stakeholders and different than the current reality.

A shared, consistent vision is a lot to ask, especially since it is being developed in the absence of reliable information. If the vision is too similar to the current reality or if people have any difficulty picturing themselves in this new reality, they will not accept or adapt to it. And, if there are conflicting visions, anyone who does change will regress if tension develops between stakeholder visions. The job of the visionary leader is to promote the shared, consistent vision among all participants.

Similarly, when a company is trying to create something new or change direction, it is best to adopt a more centralized decision and control structure. This is not the same as having one person making all decisions but is a means to facilitate the consistency that is coveted in times of change.

All too often, I have seen process-improvement efforts sputter because the infrastructure does not support the new purpose. Management is misguided if it thinks it can bolt on a process-improvement "fix" and leave everything else as it was.

Identifying the Time for Strategic Change

One of the best things you can learn from working with a startup company is the need for razor sharp strategy. You can make some money by selling just about anything for a little while, but to scale it up and to convince others to invest takes some understanding of what market you are approaching, what you have to offer, how it compares to the incumbent offering, and how you can sustain an advantage over incumbent and potential competitors. Once a company has had some success and been operating for some time, it quickly loses that strategic edge. This is not to mean that they have lost sight of the original strategy, but rather they have lost sight of the fact that the original strategy, religiously applied or not, no longer applies. And given that even small changes disrupt an overall strategy, there comes a time when a company must rethink the strategy. The competitiveness of the market will dictate how quickly a company needs to react, so depending on the competitors, a company may not even care if it has lost its strategic edge. But as long as the market is somewhat competitive, the company will have to react sooner than it would like.

Once it is clear that a change in strategy is required because a company is losing in the market, a sequence of events begins. For a while, the company will urge all of its departments to work a little harder, as if the problem is due to a drop in effort or infidelity to the original strategy. But, invariably, working harder is not enough, and it becomes clear that more of the same will not make the company better.

Typically, companies start to consider a process-improvement regime — Lean Manufacturing, Six Sigma, business process reengineering, etc. — when they realize that the status quo is not working for them, as if process-improvement regimes will solve a problem of strategy. If the thinking is "everyone should get better at the old strategy," process improvement will not save the company. And even if the company realizes that a new strategy is required, it often lacks information from operations or design to develop a new strategy. One of the benefits of process improvement (and indeed one that I push heavily in this book) is that process improvement creates clarity around operations and design so that strategic decisions can rely on operational knowledge. However, this implies that at some point there is a redirection in the process improvement from deciding what the strategy should be to implementing it. Unfortunately, management often signs up for process improvement as if it already knows what the strategy should be. They miss deciding how operations or design can contribute to a successful strategy.

Maintaining Corporate Strategy

Management may be too distant and ill-informed to generate ideas for the process improvement. That notwithstanding, management has a very important role in process improvement, and this includes keeping the initiative consistent with the current strategy. Process-improvement efforts should in no way contradict the corporate strategy. A company might decide to change its strategy on the basis of forecasts and to reflect that new strategy in a process-improvement effort, but it is bad business to train the workforce or change the workforce metrics without consciously revising the corporate strategy.

In the ordinary course, management is responsible for several elements of the corporate strategy:

- Identifying what the customer wants and how the company will respond;

- Communicating to the customer what the company hopes to deliver and how that is an appropriate response to the customer need;

- Creating a performance metrics system that recognizes (and often rewards) the right behaviour by the operators and managers;

- Recruiting the workforce that supports the corporation's customer response (at least in a general sense, to be refined by hiring managers and human resources); and

- Providing the right training and experiences for the workforce to support the customer response (honed and enforced by hiring managers and human resources).

Process-improvement decisions should not contradict any of the above elements, even if the improvement process generates previously unavailable information about the company's ability to respond to customer needs and desires.

At some point, management may decide to survey the changes that the process-improvement effort has generated and to create a new (typically more aggressive) strategy, but for the purposes of stability, in most instances management should maintain the current strategy during a process-improvement process. So, any changes in the performance metrics, staffing, tasks definition, and training should clarify the current strategy rather than change it.

Shortsightedly rewarding employees for understanding statistics, lean words, or any other distraction from the business of serving the customer should be avoided until there is clarity around the strategic benefit. Creating new positions solely for the purpose of facilitating process improvement can also be detrimental if they are not aligned with the strategy. Although creating a team to reduce defects or increase customer response can be a refinement of a current strategy (in fact those two often are), the performance metrics, the staffing, the task definitions, and the training should be keyed to the outcome and not to some artificial metric convenient for the process-improvement effort.

If the current corporate strategy is respected in the process-improvement process, engaging the front-line workers becomes simple. Management is not measuring the number of projects or the project benefit independent of the strategy but rather some metric with intrinsic strategic alignment. Rather than going to an operator or designer and saying we are looking for as many process-improvement projects as possible, we are asking them to come up with ideas to some strategic end — such as reducing defects or improving response in some specific way. They can offer valuable suggestions, and management has an interest in responding to those suggestions in whatever forum makes sense.

Which Employees to Target?

As mentioned in chapter 1, Lean Manufacturing, Six Sigma and other process-improvement regimes share tools. But there is one big difference among them: Who makes the decisions on each project? The answer to that question determines which employees to target and sets the pace and the direction of change.

Lean Manufacturing is based on the premise that the operator is the person with the biggest effect on manufacturing, and all of the lean tools focus on helping operators. So, at Toyota, getting the product to the customer in a perfect form and in the shortest possible time was affected most by operators. By contrast, Six Sigma's DMAIC focuses on the process designer or process engineer on the basis that their work creates the biggest effect. Other process-improvement regimes will focus on the front-line managers or the design of customer functions and create tools to assist them.

Different process-improvement regimes work better in different environments. Given the statistical nature of Six Sigma, it was made famous at Allied Signal, Motorola, and later General Electric — engineer-rich environments. Six Sigma works less well in environments where employees are not as familiar with statistics.

But you can only choose one focus! More than one is like more than one person steering a car — it never works.

Once you decide what class of workers your process-improvement initiative will target, implementation becomes easier, and you have more liberty to deviate from prescribed methods. With a target group, process improvement is about getting the group the best information and the best process possible to help it manage the improved journey of the part or service in question.

Too often, the people with the biggest impact on the process only see their set of tasks and don't appreciate how their work is part of something bigger. Furthermore, they feel they can't explore improvements because they are forbidden to do so or are restricted by the system. Thus, the target workers need to be empowered and encouraged to participate in the process-improvement initiative on both a formal and an informal basis. Target workers will more readily cooperate in process improvement if the company supports them and

1. Highlights what is going on with the product as far as
   • flow of product;
   • buffer levels and their purpose;

- queuing decisions;
- product inspection results; and
- process robustness.

2. Cedes control over the process to target workers and allows them to

- stop the process for analysis in the case of defects or deviation; and
- experiment with process changes.

3. Provides support to

- coordinate the efforts of different departments;
- give target workers the resources to run experiments (and potentially fail); and
- accept metrics that are meaningful to operators.

The extent to which employees can influence and improve any particular process will depend on the nature of the company's business, and even if all employees are doing their best for the company, the above list can only be applied to one group at a time — all production workers, all line supervisors, all product engineers, etc. — and cannot be shared across groups without a certain degree of conflict.

Consider the processes for getting food to a customer in a restaurant. In high-end restaurants where the food selection and variety are the selling features, the head chef usually decides product flow, queuing, quality, and any experiments and can expect help from the restaurant owner if changes are needed to the restaurant's facilities or marketing.

However, if the food offerings are more standardized, the chef may be little more than a glorified line cook, and all of the line cooks should have a say in improving the product and/or service offering in their respective areas. Having one person (the head chef) is convenient for management accountability, but does not accurately reflect the impact that the line cooks have on getting food to the customers. So, for instance, even though there may be a standard operating procedure, each line cook should have a say on how to organize their area and work flow inasmuch as best practices are not common. Experiments should be localized as much as possible and then offered farther afield if they prove successful.

In a third scenario, a restaurant may be more about the staff interaction with customers, as in a bar. In this scenario, the wait staff, who are in direct contact with customers, have the best insight on how the offering should flow. There may be issues with the food selection or how it is prepared (for which wait staff may have limited expertise), but having management support them to generate improvement ideas is more important than responding to resistance from the cooking staff. My experience at General Motors during its early attempts at Lean Manufacturing illustrate how important it is to identify and respect the focus of your improvement initiative. At Toyota, if the operator on the production line was not satisfied that the product was perfect when it left his station, they were able to (and obliged to) stop the production line. But when I worked at General Motors, the culture was such that no production manager would cede responsibility to stop the line to an operator. The thinking was that only a manager who had budgetary responsibility should be able to make a decision to stop the line. At the end of the day, the product was made right or made wrong and, budget notwithstanding, it was the operator who had the best insight into the situation. If I were consulting with a company with a culture like General Motors', the first question I would ask is "Who is the focus of the improvement?" If the focus is intended to be a line manager or production superintendent, a lot of the lean tools would not apply.

People may argue that Lean/Six Sigma (first recognized in a book of that name by Michael George) confuses the focus of process improvement because it merges Lean Manufacturing and Six Sigma, which have differing philosophies. But Lean/Six Sigma does not confuse the focus of process improvement at all. It merges the training and tools of the two regimes but does nothing to resolve who the focus should be.

When I worked at Seagate Technology, we had a large Six Sigma group and, independent of that, a Lean Manufacturing group of which I was a part. Later, I helped merge the educational components of Lean Manufacturing and Six Sigma, but in merging them we never discussed whether our focus was the operator or the engineer. We just had two groups running in parallel alternately lionizing the operator and the engineer. We did discuss how to attribute savings to the Lean Manufacturing or the Six Sigma group and decided that as long as the metrics were separated and clear, the project benefits would be recorded to both. For Lean Manufacturing the time from raw material to the customer (throughput time) was measured. For Six Sigma what was measured was the percentage of parts made from raw material to the customer on the first attempt (z-scores). We never checked how many Six Sigma projects created a longer throughput time or how many lean projects created z-score issues. (To be fair, most managers would not sign off on projects that were slow or created scrap, so such issues were managed by the process owner on an exception basis.)

But when the easy projects became scarcer, the focus of our combined educational efforts became more and more confusing. Seagate tried to resolve the confusion by merging the groups but that did not create focus.

When merging process-improvement tools, the first priority is to clarify who the target is, based on where the most strategic opportunity exists. If your target is the operator, you can use any and all tools at your disposal to support the operator. (We included lean concepts, just-in-time, Six Sigma, theory of constraints, and total quality management in our Lean Manufacturing training.) The notion is to give the operator the best opportunity to make a difference — through metrics visibility, process control, and support. On the other hand, if the process designer is your focus, you need to create metrics, process control, and support that are specific to them. Remember that only one person can drive the car. When you identify the target group early in your process-improvement initiative, you create clarity.

Sharing Improvement Lessons Within the Company

For most successful process-improvement efforts, there should be some way to share the insights gained on one project and spread the benefit across many. This is a great idea in theory but can involve practical problems. It takes time and effort to sift through project briefs that do not apply to your project or contribute to the efficiency of your project. Nevertheless, you should devise a system to catalogue your projects.

There are four good reasons to catalogue project briefs:
- Managers in the area can track, credit, and further encourage wins.

- Process-improvement champions can incorporate good ideas from other areas to their area for similar wins.
- Project managers can bring new ideas to tough problems they face.
- Project managers can hone their approach on their projects and potentially eliminate blind alleys based on similar projects in other areas.

The organization of project briefs can range from something as simple as a bulletin board that displays all projects in a haphazard arrangement to a searchable database with full files available to each user. If the knowledge base is simply a note or list of successes, set it up as an ongoing record rather than a database. (A good example of an ongoing record is a serialized file of your A3s.) Organizing it on any level other than dollars saved will not add any additional value. If a more robust use of the knowledge base is anticipated, the projects should at least have a common metric so that anyone looking at the brief has the same goal in mind. If projects don't share a common goal, they should at least be organized by outcome metric. At Seagate, when we started to merge the Lean Manufacturing and Six Sigma groups, we stored projects according to their originating regime because each regime had different metrics. Six Sigma projects typically targeted first-time-through quality or z-score, whereas Lean Manufacturing projects targeted the throughput time. Information for projects from one regime was stored in the database of the other regime as long as the project had a recognizable effect on and was structured to drive the other regime's metric. But a Lean Manufacturing project that did not affect quality served no purpose in the Six Sigma database.

Once you have decided how to organize projects among groups defined by metrics, the next thing you must decide is what content should be included in each brief. Given the list of typical uses, the only things you really need to include are the savings (to cater to the managers) and what was done (to cater to everyone else). Resist the temptation to limit the catalogue to successful attempts since those would not properly represent what was actually done on the project. In fact, you should include failed projects because they will help other project managers avoid the same mistakes.

A searchable database allows project owners elsewhere to use catalogued projects as inspiration for their own improvement initiatives and to follow a template when they implement their ideas. A searchable database also allows managers to track wins, but given the time and effort involved in creating a database, its primary purpose should not be to list successful projects. In my experience, managers usually find other ways to get the information they need about winning initiatives.

Another approach to the knowledge database is the roadshow approach. In the roadshow approach, the best projects are paraded around site to site to display the project's potential and bring acclaim to the project owners. Often, this approach will also include some archived follow-on documentation to give the roadshow message a longer life. I came across this approach in a published case called "Managing Innovation at Nypro." The innovation at this plastic injection molding company was buoyed by a competition where employees from one plant could choose projects from another plant and pay a visit to that location, ostensibly to duplicate or build the project on their own. Something similar happened at Seagate but informally. A Seagate plant in Perai, Malaysia, developed a signal system to coordinate work-in-process inventory. The system would convert existing computer screens to simple signalling agents, thus eliminating the need for operators to leave and re-enter the clean-room environment. Once other plants with similar problems heard about the new signal system, a parade of people visited Perai to replicate the system elsewhere.

Chapter 7

Statistics and Six Sigma

What makes Six Sigma harder to master than any other process-improvement regime is its use of statistics, the branch of mathematics that deals with the collection, analysis, interpretation, presentation, and organization of data. Using statistics creates a steeper learning curve. As well, it can stand in the way of communicating process-improvement results. In this section, I would like to isolate the effects and difficulties of statistics. There may be an opportunity to manage Six Sigma projects with limited statistical exposure, and a separate discussion of statistics is the only way to make that possible.

Statistics — Patterns, Not "Proof"

Statistics is the big difference between Six Sigma tools and those of other process-improvement regimes. Statistics is also one of the hardest disciplines to master. I took engineering, math, and quantitative research in university, and each time I changed programs I was given a new statistics course as if I had never taken statistics before. I was never able to opt out even though the material in each was very similar. I attribute this to the notion that nobody really learns statistics no matter how many times they take it, yet every new instructor feels that their class will finally get it.

The funny thing about statistics is how often people say they can "prove" things using statistics. The truth of the matter is that if you can "prove" something, you do not need statistics — you can prove it directly.

You often hear people say that numbers do not lie. It's true: If I survey the 10 people in my department and 8 want pepperoni pizza and 2 want just cheese, that represents the truth. However, if someone says that the trend is towards cheese pizza, there should really be a discussion around who was surveyed on which occasions and under which conditions because this statistic is not self-evident.

Think of it this way. If there are direct ways to approach a problem, a direct approach can and should be used. Only when all direct ways have been exhausted can statistics be used to make generalizations. As the word suggests, generalizations cannot answer questions about specific occurrences. They can only provide simplified overviews because once we admit that we do not know the answer, we have to resort to pattern recognition, and that's where statistics are effective. But we're not "proving" anything with statistics.

Consider a rudderless boat going down rapids. It is out of control and at the whim of the currents. I'm not able to predict where the boat will go in the river, nor can I control it. However, I know that the boat will be in the river at any point along its journey. And, statistically, if I have to guess where the boat is in relation to either shore, I will be wrong by the least distance if I guess the middle of the river. That's because the middle is the closest to all of the other points in the cross-section of the river, not because I have any special insights about the boat or its position. Given this bit of statistical logic, one might say they know the boat is in the middle of the river — or worse, they know with enough samples that the boat will trend toward the middle of the river and they can "control" it this way. But those conclusions would be wrong. The boat will be wherever it is in the river, and no amount of statistics that will change that. Minimizing statistical errors may make the observer feel better, but it won't help anyone on the boat!

Statistics, at its heart, is very straightforward. You look for a pattern and decide if what you see fits that pattern. The problem is that the "pattern" is represented in mathematical terms, and people often do not have a sufficient enough grasp of mathematics to understand and interpret the way those patterns are represented. For a further discussion about the principles of statistics, I have included an exercise called the "3-Card Statistical Exercise" (see page 141) that I use to teach high school students. However, it should be clear to anyone uncomfortable with statistics that there are drawbacks to introducing statistical-based process improvements. It should be equally clear to anyone comfortable using statistics that what they find easy is not necessarily easy for others.

Keeping Statistics in Perspective

When a company decides on a process-improvement regime that involves statistics, all participants need to have a solid understanding of relevant statistical concepts. That understanding is a necessary condition for successful implementation. But grasping the principles of statistics isn't enough. Participants also have to appreciate what the process-improvement project is about and what it is intended to accomplish. Only then can they make sure that statistics is used in the service of the project and not the other way around.

The most common shortcut in Six Sigma is to omit a discussion of what is the right or wrong approach for the project because some employees have a difficulty with statistics. When statistics becomes the focus of a project, the culture quickly polarizes, and tribes form — those who can do mathematics and those who may have a better understanding of the project but struggle with the math. In my experience, the math is less important than a notional understanding of what is going on in the project, even though statistics gets the most attention in implementation.

You would think that statistical process-improvement regimes would be better suited to engineering cultures, engineers being more likely to understand mathematics. In those cultures, the polarization of who can or cannot do the math is more pronounced, but people still need to be able to get beyond the basic math and understand the project on a conceptual level. To keep the statistical aspects of process improvement in perspective, a project has to be led by someone who gets both the mathematics and the notional concept and who can reinforce both on a regular and visible basis. Without this leadership, Six Sigma implementations often become a statistical training program for the sake of understanding statistics and return very little in the way of true process improvement.

Six Sigma Practice Tip 1 — Define Defects Well at the Outset

In Define, Measure, Analyze, Improve, and Control (DMAIC, a Six Sigma methodology), the first step is defining the defect, and it usually isn't difficult for a trained Black Belt to find a metric for that purpose. For example, if I am looking at a bottle filling operation in a juice factory, I can either use the height of the column of juice or the weight of the juice in the bottle to help me understand if the bottle was filled with the right volume of juice. Since the amount of juice that can be put in the bottle depends on natural phenomena — human response, air pressure, specific gravity of the fluid, agitation, etc. — I can also assume that it will follow a normal probability curve. Therefore, the key to minimizing the defect of over- or under-filled bottles is understanding how to affect the mean and standard deviation through input variables. The input variables will depend on whether the process is manual or automated, but the patterns of good and defective outputs are pretty straightforward.

The problem arises when the Black Belt defines the defect as "less than optimal" without specifying the specific pattern that is associated with that definition. There is no doubt that "optimum" will be defined at a later stage, but the risk is that different patterns will be used in other parts of the project, resulting in inconsistent approaches. In the juice filling example, if the Black Belt chose column height in one experiment and weight in another, they may run into problems when the density of the juice changes due to pulp or other factors. So, this seemingly subtle difference can have a big impact on the effectiveness of the project. At the design stage, the Black Belt should have chosen one unit of measure only so that the definition of a defect is clear and consistent throughout the project.

Six Sigma Practice Tip 2 — Use the Right Statistical Method

I once interviewed for a Black Belt position, and the Master Black Belt interviewing me mentioned a project where he was looking at the number of defects that occurred and had used parametric statistics to stabilize the process. That method was wrong. When you count things (like defects), the output does not follow a normal distribution for two main reasons: Counting numbers are lower bound (you can't have a negative number of defects) and some defects mask or create other defects, making the counting of them imperfect. Looking for a normal distribution pattern does not make sense if the phenomenon will not generate something like a normal distribution, so other patterns must be used. (It is possible that by coincidence you are working in the right direction of improvement despite the wrong approach, but your ability to improve efficiently and eventually control the process is hampered.) Given that this was an interview, I thought the Master Black Belt was testing me to see if I knew the difference between parametric and nonparametric statistics, so I dutifully pointed out the flaw in his approach. The interview then became a bit uncomfortable. I realized that rather than testing me, he (a certified Master Black Belt) did not know the difference between these statistical methods.

In Six Sigma training, Black Belts do a statistical test to check if the output they see from the process follows a normal distribution. The idea is that if it does, they assume it to be parametric phenomena; they assume the output pattern for comparison is the normal distribution. This is wrong. Normal distributions come from natural, relatively unbounded phenomena like how tall people are or how much an egg weighs. If you are capturing lengths or weights, you are generally correct to assume a normal distribution. In the 3-card example, I used parametric statistics only after showing that the specific pattern I was looking for was representative. Counting or accumulation does not typically result in a normal distribution, and if your output looks that way, it might just be a coincidence that will later cause you trouble.

Imposing a normal distribution where it doesn't belong is a common problem. It often occurs when mathematical prowess is assigned a higher priority than understanding general statistical principles. Even when grading students in my teaching days, the administration would regularly ask us to "bell" marks so that the class distribution resembled the normal distribution, yet would warn us to adjust any contentious marks up or down (like a 49% grade when a passing grade is 50%). The issue was that students' understanding of the course material did not lend itself to a normal distribution but often followed multimodal distributions. It was the administration that forced the distribution to be normal and then to corrupt the pattern through "adjustments." If I were studying marks in a school, I would likely use nonparametric statistics even though the output "looked parametric."

Six Sigma Practice Tip 3 — Make Sure You Can Get Good Data

There is a push to move Six Sigma from its traditional roots in manufacturing and design to transactional or service applications. I am all for this change, as I feel that Six Sigma adds nuances and rigour that are not available through other process-improvement regimes. However, Six Sigma certification that applies to manufacturing may not be appropriate for situations where many of the projects not only require a nonparametric approach but require primary data gathering because the metrics that need to be improved don't yet exist (let alone have a data store).

Let me walk you through a fictitious project at an order desk. Let's say the desk has 10 employees who take customer orders for computer hardware over the phone. Data like the average time per call or sales per call can be readily acquired through the computer tracking system, so one might think that Six Sigma is an appropriate improvement regime. These data make it fairly easy to identify certain improvements — calls should be reduced from an average of 3 minutes to an average of 2 minutes, 40 seconds to increase the response rate, sales per call should be increased from $28 to $30 to increase revenue, the main product should be hyped on calls from key customers to increase the hit rate from 1 in 10 calls to 1 in 4, and so forth. However, once you realize that better dashboards and training for staff would have the biggest impact, you quickly see that the data you need to track is not captured — how often phrases get mentioned, what products naturally sell with other products, and which calls are for sales and which are for information. In many instances, that data needs to be researched from scratch. Presenting the data that exists will at best offer descriptive statistics (and indicate if something went wrong) but will never offer normative statistics (and indicate the direction of improvement) until primary research is introduced.

Six Sigma Practice Tip 4 — Have the Right Number of Samples

Sample size is often covered in Black Belt training. However, I have seen situations where at the outset it was clear that the project would require so much sampling that the Six Sigma methodology would be too cumbersome. As mentioned above, a shift towards service applications of Six Sigma has created a data crisis because most of the metrics that lead to improvement in the service industry are not captured.

Let's go back to the call centre and assume that we want shorter calls so we can do more of them — that metric exists, and we have a store of data. Assume as well that we want more calls with revenue associated to a call and that those data exist too. However, if we were to start a project in call time reduction or call closing, we would encounter a dearth of data for what inputs lead to a shorter call or sales other than what type of call, who called, or who responded. Projects in our new areas of enquiry tend to be of two types: obvious or ridiculously time consuming.

The "obvious" projects will identify the "best worker" and point out that they should get more work or others should be more like them. The relevant data for these projects exist, and they will go off without a hitch in fairly short order. Statistical rigour may help articulate that one employee is better, but it really comes down to management 101: Have your best people on the most important things, and if you find that you were wrong about your best people, adjust accordingly. Unless the process is so opaque or disputed that statistics is the only way to analyze it, this should never be a Black Belt project for anything more than a training discussion.

That leaves the "ridiculously time consuming" category. In order to include input variables that are not normally tracked, we have to accept that it may take a lot of time to capture new metrics only to find that they are not important. Sometimes, it is just easier to assume something is important based on anecdotal evidence instead of statistical rigour and see what benefit comes from changing it. This dilemma is made worse by the structure of the DMAIC process and the need for power in statistics (power here means that enough samples were used so that the outcome is statistically significant). Often the best Six Sigma route through the mire is a design-of-experiment methodology that helps determine the relationship between factors affecting a process and the output. In such a methodology, as we collect data, we refine what we are trying to gain from them and change the experiment accordingly. This sounds great in theory but it is the most complicated thing you can do in statistics and is not for the statistically faint of heart. Furthermore, this is the very situation that grassroots lean was developed for in that the real issue is a lack of visibility as to what is important. Setup reduction or visual factory should be applied first to aid in the understanding of the process, but they do not lend themselves well to Six Sigma structures such as DMAIC.

Process Improvement Through Statistics

When an executive sells the idea of using statistics to improve processes, the audience doesn't see the depth required. However, the implementation of statistics as a process-improvement tool (be it statistical process control or Six Sigma) involves all of the complexity in a simple statistical exercise and often much more!

The most common shortcut in a Six Sigma improvement is for people to dismiss the notional discussion of what is the right approach or wrong approach and hang their expertise on the fact that they can accurately calculate the statistics. The culture quickly polarizes between the two camps: those who can do the mathematics (misapplied statistics notwithstanding) and those who struggle with the terms mean and standard deviation (but potentially better understand the projects). The math is less important than the notional understanding of what is going on even though it gets the most focus in implementation. You would think that statistical process-improvement regimes would likely be better applied to engineering cultures (engineers being more likely to have an understanding of mathematics). I typically notice in these quantitative cultures that the polarization of who can or cannot do the math is more pronounced but the benefits of people being able to get beyond the basic math to the notional concepts is about the same. The program leader has to both get the mathematics and the notional concept and enforce them on a regular and visible basis. Without this leading from above, Six Sigma implementations often become a statistical training program for the sake of understanding statistics and return very little in the way of true process improvement.

Statistics for Transactional Projects

There is a push to move Six Sigma from its traditional roots in manufacturing and design into transactional or service applications. I am all for this as I feel the tool adds nuances and rigour not available through other process-improvement regimes. However, as you move away from manufacturing projects, the use of parametric statistics drops off considerably. The problem of misrepresenting non-parametric projects only gets worse. Furthermore, Six Sigma certification applied to manufacturing may not be appropriate for situations where many of the projects not only require a non-parametric approach but require primary data gathering because the metrics that need to be improved don't yet exist (let alone have a data store).

Let me explain by walking you through a fictitious project at an order desk. The order desk has 10 employees taking customer orders over the phone for computer hardware. Data like the average time per call as well as sales per call can be readily acquired through the computer tracking system (as well as many other numbers) so one might think this setup would be an apt application of Six Sigma. These data make it fairly easy when defining the problem (call length should be reduced from an average of 3 minutes to an average of 2 minutes and 40 seconds to increase the response rate; sales per call should be increased from $28 per call to $30 per call to increase revenue; the main product should be hyped on calls from key customers to increase the hit rate from 1 in 10 calls buying the product to 1 in 4). However, once you realize that the biggest impact you have is on better dashboards and training for your staff, you quickly realize that the data you need to track (such as how often phrases get mentioned, what products naturally sell with other products, and which calls are for sales and which are for information) are not captured. Many cases need to be researched from scratch. Not only is this task difficult (even for someone who has invested a lot of time in statistical rigour), but once the data are observed we realize that they are non-parametric. As well, where manufacturing data of all types are usually ubiquitous, we now have to get our own data manually and need exceedingly high sample sizes to make it rigorous. In a situation like this one, a visual factory approach is often the best first project.

Six Sigma is a sophisticated tool that will provide definitive answers to some very complicated problems. However, anything short of an engineering culture is likely ill-suited for this approach and the extra rigour afforded comes at the expense of large, inflexible projects.

Having a comprehensive and progressive corporate strategy is essential to a successful process-improvement implementation. However, as much as it is essential, it is not sufficient. To have a successful process-improvement implementation, the corporate strategy has to be translated into an operations strategy and then refined to identify the new operations metrics that have the most impact. Only in applying the process-improvement effort to these few metrics (and the select few departments that affect these metrics) can a corporate-wide process-improvement implementation be successful.

Appendix 1

The Statistical Weakness of Six Sigma

3-Card Statistical Exercise

I have taught high school classes at the senior level in data management. This course introduces the students to statistics. As much as the prescribed curriculum jumps into calculating some statistical parameters (like mean and standard deviation), I don't think that introducing these parameters out of context makes any sense. I use a simple card technique to show the value and limitations of statistics and to tie statistics back to probability.

I divide the class into three groups, although you could have more. I take a standard card deck and hand one group the cards ace to 10 of spades, one group ace to 10 of clubs, and one group ace to 10 of hearts. I then have each group deal 3 cards, add them (the ace, A, = 1) and put the sum on the board. So if a group deals a 6, a 4, and an A, the sum would be 6+4+1 or 11. I have them repeat this 50 times and keep track of the 50 sums for the 50 trios of cards they draw. I then have them create a histogram (a graph symbolically showing how many of each sum they get) so that at the end I have 3 separate lists and 3 separate histograms on the board for discussion (see pages 144 and 145). The histogram is meant to be a proxy for the probability distribution function or an indicator of how relatively likely a sum will occur.

The students will all have taken some classes in probability at this point. They will likely not be comfortable creating a probability distribution graph for this situation at this point in the class but I have created a graph of the distribution function for possible outcomes for a 3-sample sum of cards A-10 here (see page 142).

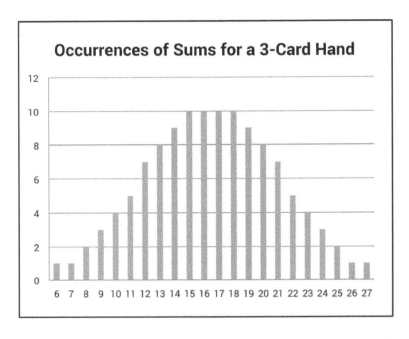

As the graph shows, there is only one way the trio of cards could add up to 6 (A+2+3); there is only one way the trio of cards could add up to 7 (A+2+4); there are two ways the sum could add up to 8 (A+2+5 and A+3+4); ... 10 ways to add up to 15 and so on until there is only one way to add up to 27 (8+9+10). There are 120 equally likely possibilities for the outcome of three cards selected from a 10-card deck so we can calculate the probability (the number of occurrences in any one column divided by the 120 to get the percentage of the chance of getting the number in that column). This new graph with probability percentages instead of occurrences is called the probability distribution function (see page 143).

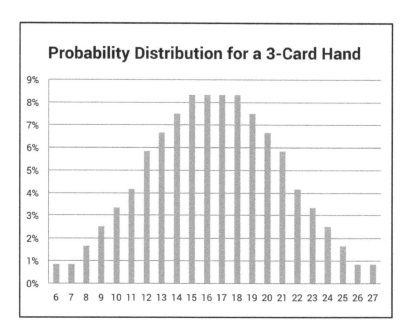

Looking at this graph, there is roughly a 4% chance of getting the sum of 11 when drawing 3 cards from a 10-card deck. There is no unique highest probability for this graph but you can see that getting a sum of 15, 16, 17, or 18 for the trio is more likely than any other sum. Again, the students will have a notion of this but may not be able to create this graph. In that regard, they would be in the same situation as the average person reading this book. They do, however, know how to create a histogram — a record of what numbers they observe ordered by their sums. (See page 145 for the histograms by group showing a typical outcome for three groups of students each doing 50 trios.)

Typical Outcome for 50 3-Card Sums

Spades	Clubs	Hearts
14	18	19
11	11	19
17	16	13
26	25	18
14	19	12
23	23	14
26	18	11
12	13	18
15	24	10
18	26	18
9	18	18
16	12	16
16	13	12
23	9	19
13	21	20
13	13	16
20	17	16
20	19	15
23	19	21
13	17	16
9	16	18
18	19	8
23	17	17
13	14	12
20	19	13
17	13	23
14	13	11
9	19	20
15	10	18
19	15	10
22	16	12
19	15	16
10	16	16
17	19	25
15	17	10
13	22	17
20	20	15
21	21	14
16	16	26
17	18	13
10	21	11
17	18	20
18	13	27
15	22	12
18	17	14
14	20	20
15	12	18
19	25	18

Actual occurrences for each group

	Spades	Clubs	Hearts
6	0	0	0
7	0	0	0
8	0	0	1
9	3	1	0
10	2	1	3
11	1	1	3
12	1	2	5
13	5	6	3
14	4	1	3
15	5	2	2
16	3	5	7
17	5	5	2
18	4	5	8
19	3	8	3
20	4	2	4
21	1	3	1
22	1	2	0
23	5	1	1
24	0	1	0
25	0	2	1
26	2	1	1
27	0	0	1

Occurrences grouped by sum from 6 to 27

16.69388	17.40816	16.14286	mean	16.5
4.378946	3.968198	4.25245	standard deviation	

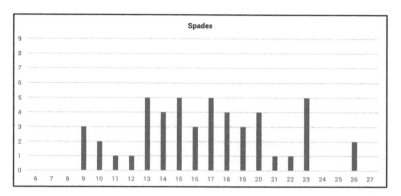

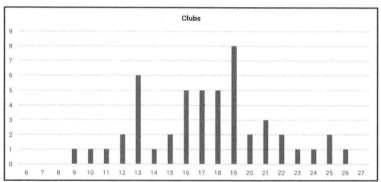

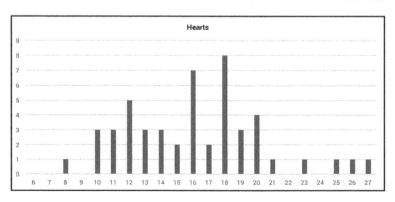

Once this information (or something similar) is on the board in the classroom, I ask the students why the distributions look similar and why they look different. You will notice that none of them look like the probability distribution function; this is because so few samples (50) were taken. The real benefit of statistics is to be able to identify when different data sets represent the same phenomena or different phenomena. To their responses I inquire if the different distributions represent different phenomena. I play on the fact that they did "seemingly" the same thing but got different averages and different standard deviations representing very different distributions. They assert that the phenomena observed are the same because all groups have essentially the same set of cards and any difference in output is just natural randomness. I further inquire as to if the clubs group did something different given that their distribution did not seem as flat as the other two groups. (I note that the mean or average is the highest of the three groups and the standard deviation is the lowest of the three.) The class insists that the processes were fundamentally the same so any differences are a result of random variation or noise. In a last attempt to isolate the clubs distribution, I ask how much difference in the outcome would be required to convince the class that the different distributions represent different phenomena, to which they glibly respond, "We would need to see more of a difference than is shown here given that we did the exact same thing."

You will notice that none of the histograms look exactly like the probability distribution function or each other. Ideally they will trend toward the probability distribution function but dissimilarities are common, especially at relatively low sample sizes. It is for this reason that we do not typically rely on the human eye to spot the differences but rather use statistical parameters.

Since there will always be differences across outcomes of the same phenomena, what I am really asking them is, What good is statistics? If you are willing to accept any level of difference across distributions as the same (represented by histograms and parameters), how can statistics possibly be effective at finding potential differences? To put a finer point on it: If someone had dropped a card from their deck so that it was not part of their distribution, would you be able to tell and how?

I then reveal to the class that I tricked them by withholding the 3 of clubs. Hearts and spades had the distribution I had indicated but the deck of clubs had only 9 cards — A, 2, 4, 5, 6, 7, 8, 9, and 10. When I explain, the groups will typically still have their cards, so they quickly inspect their decks to see that the spades and hearts decks are complete but the clubs deck is indeed missing the 3. (It is important to have them verify this omission: By letting them inspect an unadulterated deck, they can be sure I am telling the truth despite often being in denial that the trick was even played!) I then repeat my earlier questions — specifically whether we can discern if the distributions represented different phenomena, to which many individuals turn to teammates to say, "I told you so — I knew they were different!" I reset the discussion by noting that if they could not articulate what threshold was required to indicate different phenomena, they must be rationalizing their observations to create congruence with the new information. This is less statistics than revisionist history.

I use this example to indicate that this type of discussion is the very reason why we have statistics. This rationale is the very thing that statistics is supposed to tell us, but when the information is laid out in front of us we still can't tell. Here is a situation where we know what pattern we are looking for and we have an example (clubs) where we know the pattern should not fit. I show the probability distribution for a 3-card-hand sum in each case with the complete deck centred around 16.42 and the clubs deck without the 3 centred around 17.17 (see page 148). (If students have questions, it is well within the scope of the class to show how these distributions were generated.)

Statistics can be quite unintuitive; consider how people will look at the first output of 50 sums and debate whether they can find a difference or not even though there are not nearly enough samples. This example is a clear illustration of the complexities of using statistics.

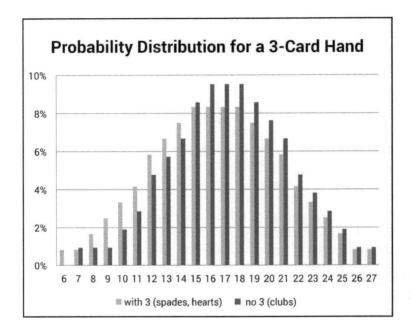

Appendix 2

Lean Tools — How and Why

How	Why
A3 — This tool's name refers to A3 paper size (29.7 x 42 cm or roughly 11 x 17 inches). The intention is to summarize the project on one sheet of paper so that it is succinct and approachable on the first read.	A3 — Creating a summary or abstract for each project is useful for archiving and reference. At Seagate we also used this type of "one-page" project presentation as a slide-presentable document to credit the people running the project.
Kanban — The name comes from a Japanese term meaning *signal* or *card*. Production is scheduled on a pull basis where the signal for production is a card, empty parking spot, empty tote, or other mobile artefact that is only issued to production when the last part has been used.	Kanban — This tool primarily implements pull scheduling so that schedule asymmetries do not result in inventory buildup. As much as kanban is used to reduce inventory as it relates to imperfect scheduling, it is often seen as an impediment to further inventory reduction as its nature is to have inventory available. In later stages of process improvement, it is often replaced with something better.

How	Why
Error Proofing (Poka-Yoke) — This sequence of steps identifies errors that contribute to defects and compares them to red flags that confound operators, in an attempt to eliminate those errors.	Error Proofing (Poka-Yoke) — Defects are related to potential errors and those errors are addressed in such a way as to eliminate their possibility.
Fishbone Diagram (Ishikawa Diagram) — Errors associated with a specific defect (the head of the fish) are organized in categories for completeness and association (the bones of the fish).	Fishbone Diagram (Ishikawa Diagram) — This graphical approach is used to recognize patterns in errors that contribute to a specific defect in an attempt to isolate it.
5S — The term refers to 5 Japanese words (often translated as Sort, Straighten, Shine, Standardize, and Sustain) that convert an operational environment to its bare minimum. It can be summarized as "a place for everything and everything in its place."	5S — Many of the 7 wastes are generated because of a poor operational environment. 5S is a way to directly make the operational environment waste-free. Operational managers often get distracted and think that 5S is a way to justify cleaning an area and making it more presentable. The effort involved does not justify the aesthetics and should be reserved for waste elimination.
Design-of-Experiments (DOE) — In this iterative approach, early experiments look for coarse effects that later inform experiments to refine the approach.	Design-of-Experiments (DOE) — This method breaks down complicated phenomena through waves of experiments that successively narrow in scope.

How	Why
Suggestion Program — The main idea is to give employees who can best improve the operations, and anyone who can help them, a channel to feed half-baked ideas to those employees who can develop them. By setting up convenient suggestion boxes (an email address is likely the most current version of a "box"), employees can submit suggestions as ideas come to them. Typically the better suggestions generate rewards on the order of 10% of the first-year savings. A problem is that not all savings are monetary, so companies can offer a separate prize for good suggestions (like safety suggestions or otherwise) that cannot easily be monetized.	Suggestion Program — More a gauge of employee participation than a lean tool, it has found its way into the lean canon. A big part of the original Toyota Production System, it was copied with limited success in the North American auto industry. The interest in it has waned, likely because it is hard for consultants to package and sell. The real strength of suggestion programs is that management can express what they see as good and usable ideas (to be copied) versus unexecutable random thoughts.
Value-Stream Mapping — Much like process mapping, but it includes such lean metrics as cycle time, setup time, and manufacturing cycle time.	Value-Stream Mapping — A wonderful starting point for project mining because it highlights all the places where better coordination is possible and allows for a baseline comparison.
Going to the Gemba — Quite literally means going to where the work is done.	Going to the Gemba — Regular operations immersion is essential to root-cause analysis and supports thoughtful consideration of ongoing projects.

How	Why
Hoshin Kanri — The practice of upper management clarifying desired outcomes and leaving it to their direct reports to propose objectives and objective measures for their performance metrics.	Hoshin Kanri — Essentially is management by objectives. Supports a process of "catchball" where subordinates propose and work with management to define the performance metric system.
ABC Inventory Analysis – Considers that high, steady movers in inventory (A items), high but infrequent movers (B items), and slow movers (C items) need to be classified separately. Typically the top 80% of expenditures on an annual basis can be attributed to 20% of the items.	ABC Inventory Analysis – Allows management to focus on the inventory items that need most attention so that projects can be scoped based on need.
Setup Reduction – This organized approach lists all tasks that need to be executed in order to set up the equipment for its next production run. The steps are categorized as unnecessary, necessary but not value-added, and value-added. The first category steps are removed from the sequence. The second are analyzed for modification. The third are shrunk where possible.	Setup Reduction – Reduces regular and repetitive activities. Originally applied to readying equipment for production runs but can be applied to any regular sequence of steps, such as product approvals, employee processing, and transaction clearing. The benefits of setup reduction are often underestimated because the impact on inventory levels or wait times is often hard to recognize.
Cross-functional Teams –The practice of inviting other stakeholders into the project execution process.	Cross-functional Teams – Help break down silos in organizations and are essential to looking up- and downstream beyond the current area of improvement.

How	Why
Visual Factory – The collection of practices including 5S, posting station information, andon lights, and general workplace organization.	Visual Factory – The environment is curated so that all visual cues direct operators and managers to see the current operational state and positively affect it.
Shadow Board – Made by creating a silhouette of each item stored on the board so that its location can be easily identified whether it is there or not. The shadow board also highlights anything that is misplaced.	Shadow Board – This device organizes tools or consumables. It operates much like a checklist when applied to kitting or cleanup but also helps identify missing or misplaced items.
Xbar-R Chart – A time-series capture of product characteristics that are either gauged or manually recorded by the operator. The graph will typically have an upper-control-limit line and a lower-control-limit line that indicate when the process needs attention.	Xbar-R Chart – Often assumed to be associated with defects, the chart does not actually measure the part as much as process consistency (control limits do not necessarily indicate a defect). The benefit of the chart is to indicate when the process is behaving or not behaving in an expected way.

Acknowledgements

This book is a result of (among other things) two positive periods in my life. The first was working at Ernst & Young in the late 1990s; I got to work with some exceptional people of all stripes and I honed my aptitude for process improvement and helping others. Cameron Hay, Don Hambly, Larry D'Andrea and Charlie Reid were invaluable in my development and worth special mention as mentors as it relates to this book. The second period was working at Seagate Technology; I was part of a crack team deployed to extend process improvement around the world. Many people there deserve credit for the thoughts, discussions and accomplishments that are the basis of this book. However, I have to give special recognition to the team of Sue Gillman, Shannon Randall, Mike Verdin and Richard Craven (I was the wackiest member) for achieving a level of global lean success I would never have thought possible. Not only did we achieve lean success on three continents and with a variety of manufacturing technologies, but we wrote the script that anyone could follow. This book is little more than an homage to those periods in my life and the people who helped me understand process improvement.